A Soul Remembers

HIROSHIMA

by

Dolores Cannon

OZARK MOUNTAIN PUBLISHERS

P.O. Box 754

Huntsville, AR 72740-0754

For permission, or serialization, condensation, adaptions, or for our catalog of other publications, write to Ozark Mountain Publishers, Attn.: Permission Department, P.O. Box 754, Huntsville, AR 72740-0754.

Library of Congress Cataloging-in-Publication Data
Cannon, Dolores, 1931–
    A Soul Remembers Hiroshima by Dolores Cannon
    A case of reincarnation, where a young American girl relives the life and death of a Japanese man through regressive hypnosis.
1. Hypnosis 2. Reincarnation 3. Past-life therapy   4. Atomic bomb
5. World War II   6. Hiroshima   7. Japan
I. Cannon, Dolores, 1931– II. Atomic Bomb III. World War II
IV. Title
Library of Congress Catalog Card Number: 92-083932
ISBN 0-9632776-6-9

Cover Design: Joe Alexander
Book set in Adobe Minion & Medici Script
Book Design: Kris Kleeberg

Published by:

OZARK MOUNTAIN PUBLISHERS

P.O. Box 754

Huntsville, AR 72740-0754

Printed in United States of America

Table of Contents

Books by Dolores Cannon

Conversations with Nostradamus, Volume I
Conversations with Nostradamus, Volume II
Conversations with Nostradamus, Volume III
Jesus and the Essenes
Keepers of the Garden
Conversations with a Spirit
A Soul Remembers Hiroshima

Conversations with Nostradamus is available
in abridged form on audio tape cassette.

Forthcoming books by Dolores Cannon

They Walked with Jesus
Five Lives Remembered
Star Crash

For more information about any
of the above titles, or other titles
in our catalog, write to:

OZARK MOUNTAIN PUBLISHERS

P.O. Box 754
Huntsville, AR 72740-0754

Wholesale Inquiries Welcome

I am become Death,

The shatterer of worlds.

—Bhagavad Gita
*(Quoted by J. Robert Oppenheimer while
recalling the first atomic bomb blast near
Alamogordo, NM, July 16, 1945.)*

KEY TO THE COVER

(Drawn from newspaper pictures during the historic event.)

1. *Albert Einstein, the scientist whose equation $E = mc^2$ caused the world of physicists to ponder how to release the energy locked within matter, thus creating destructive forces on a hitherto undreamed-of scale.*
2. *"Little Boy," the nuclear bomb that destroyed Hiroshima.*
3. *Japanese crying as they listened to Emperor Hirohito on the wireless, announcing that the Empire was surrendering.*
4. *"The Atomic Dome," formerly the Industrial Promotion Hall, in Hiroshima, which has been left in ruins as a reminder of the event.*
5. *The mushroom cloud created by "Little Boy" as it fell on Hiroshima.*
6. *Colonel Paul Tibbets waves from his ship Enola Gay just before taking off to drop the fatal bomb.*
7. *One of the corpses left at the scene. Other people were totally disintegrated.*
8. *A Japanese woman digs through the rubble of her house in Hiroshima.*
9. *United States' President Harry Truman, who gave the final order to drop the bomb.*
10. *A Japanese watch which stopped operating at 8:15 A.M., when blasted by the shock wave from the bomb.*
11. *Little baby, Kathryn Harris, who was born with the memories of the experience in her subconscious.*

Preface

I WAS A CHILD in World War II and my memories of it are colored by a child's point of view. I remember the American response to the sneak attack at Pearl Harbor was to look upon the Japanese as monsters without souls. And I remember the celebrations on VJ (Victory in Japan) day, following the bombings of Hiroshima and Nagasaki.

Nogorigatu Suragami was an elderly man who was in Hiroshima on that fateful day in 1945 when the "Enola Gay" dropped its atomic payload on that Japanese city. I "met" him only recently—more than 40 years after his death.

Nogorigatu was just one of many personalities I discovered during the hypnotic regression of a young woman I happened to meet at a party. As a past life researcher, I have conducted hundreds of hypnotic sessions—enough to convince me of the validity of reincarnation and the multiple lives most of us have led. But never had I faced a challenge that an entity like Nogorigatu would present.

My primary goal, as a researcher, is to remain always objective, reporting the facts as they occur, without emotion. Nogorigatu's story would test that goal, as well as shake several long-held beliefs, before reaching its tragic conclusion.

Nogorigatu's words, coming from a petite young woman, revealed him to be a kind, caring, intelligent, witty and charming man. I considered him my friend and, I would learn, he thought the same of me. Listening as he described his own death, amid cries of fear and confusion, was not easy and it affected me deeply.

There have been many stories of pain, death and destruction told by survivors of the Hiroshima bombing. This is the eyewitness account of one who did *not* survive.

Dolores Cannon

Chapter 1

The Beginning of the Adventure

"*I* KNOW YOU FROM SOMEWHERE, don't I?" I said as I was introduced to the pretty young girl. "Where have we met?"

As we gazed into each other's eyes, she sensed it too. It was an instant recognition, an instant "knowing." As we talked, we realized that it was impossible. We couldn't have met before, because she had only recently moved to our area from Texas.

The year was 1983. I was attending a party given by friends interested in metaphysics and psychic phenomena and Kathryn Harris had come with one of her friends. After racking my brain, common sense prevailed and I had to agree it was the first time we had met. Still, as I watched her circulate around the room infecting everyone with her contagious personality, I could not shake the feeling that I knew her. She seemed so familiar.

Whether this feeling was triggered by past-life memories of another time when we might have been acquainted or a premonition of our future association together, I will never know. I only know that our meeting at that party must have been preordained, because it was the beginning of an incredible adventure together.

Neither of us had any way of knowing what was to occur during the next year. I know now that we were destined to work together and meeting at the party was the first step along the path into the unknown—a path from which there was no turning back.

I had begun regressive hypnotic research into past lives in 1979 and had worked with hundreds of eager and willing subjects. During that time, I had no idea I would ever find someone like Kathryn who, with her incredible capacity to provide detail, would turn out to be a researcher's dream.

When the talk on the evening of our introduction turned to the work that I was doing, many people expressed curiosity and wanted to make appointments to explore their past lives. Kathryn was one of these and as we set up the date, I had no idea she would be any different from the many others I had worked with.

Kathryn, or Katie, as she was known to her friends, was only 22 years old then. She was short and rather buxom for her age, with close-cut blond hair and sparkling blue eyes that seemed to penetrate beneath the surface of others. Radiating charisma out of every pore of her skin, she seemed so happy and alive, so interested in people. (I discovered later, through our association, that often this was a façade to cover her basic shyness and insecurity. She was a Cancer, after all, and people born under that astrological sign are usually not that gregarious.)

But Kathryn had a sincerity about her, an innate sense of wisdom that belied her true age. At times, when signs of immaturity would come through, it seemed out of place. I had to keep reminding myself that she was only 22—the same age as my own son, though the two were nothing alike. She seemed like a very old soul in a deceivingly young body. I wondered if anyone else got the same impression.

Kathryn was born in Los Angeles in 1960 to parents whose jobs required extensive travel and frequent moves. They were members of a pentecostal church, so Katie's religious background was certainly not one that would encourage thoughts of reincarnation and hypnosis. She said she had always felt out of place in this family, and her parents couldn't understand her reluctance to be like them.

It was mostly out of concern for her parents' feelings that she asked to be anonymous in this book. She felt they would never understand the idea of many lives, even though it was an easy concept for her to grasp. She also didn't want to risk the possibility that her private life would be upset. I have agreed to respect her wishes and keep her identity a secret.

Her family's many moves through various states finally brought them to Texas when Katie was 16. Forced to relocate twice in her sophomore year in high school and again at the beginning of her junior year, Katie was tired of constantly adjusting to new schools, different teaching methods and temporary friends. Over the protests of her parents, she dropped out of school early in her junior year, ending her formal education. This was to become an asset in our work. Katie is an extremely intelligent girl, but her knowledge did not come from books.

Once out of school, and with apparent freedom, Katie discovered she couldn't find work easily without a high school diploma or specialized training. After a year of disappointingly menial jobs, she decided, at 17, to take a high school equivalency exam and later joined the Air Force where she spent two years specializing in computers. (An important point for our work was that she never left the United States during her time with the Air Force.)

After leaving the service, she and her family moved a final time to the midwestern city where I met her. Using her computer skills in office work, Katie seems well adjusted and has a normal social life. The extent of her spare time is spent reading popular romance and fantasy novels. The idea of researching in a library for historical or geographical information would not appeal to her at all.

When Kathryn Harris and I first met, neither of us had any idea of the adventure we were embarking upon. It was to continue for an entire year and encompass time periods and experiences beyond imagination. At the party, she was just one of many who had expressed curiosity about hypnotic regressions into past lives. These regressions, for me, had fallen into a predictable pattern and it seemed the more I did, the more predictable the outcome became. I had no reason to expect anything different from this vivacious, enthusiastic young girl as I set up our first appointment.

Generally in the first hypnotic session, the vast majority of people will only enter lighter trance states. This is where the predictable patterns come in. They recount a dull, boring, everyday life where nothing exciting happened—just every-day events similar to those that occur in most of our lives.

For some reason, many will return to a life in the Old West, during the pioneer and early settlement days. Though there seems to be an attraction to that time period, all hypnotic subjects report something different from what they have been exposed to all their lives in movies and TV programs, and many have remarked on this. When these differences are consistent among the subjects, verifying each other's stories in their description of the areas and time periods, it proves, to me, the validity of reincarnation while providing what I believe to be a truer picture of history.

I have formed my own opinion of why these first sessions follow specific patterns. I believe when the subject relates an uneventul life, it is because his subconscious mind is testing either him or me. The subject doesn't really know me, making the subconscious reluctant to reveal important, innermost secrets to a stranger.

This is also a new experience for the subject and while my method can induce the subconscious to release information, it is still the guardian of that information. Because its role is primarily one of protection, the subconscious will choose something easy—a simple life from its many files—to see how the subject will react. It is almost as though it is saying, "Well, we don't really know what's going on here, but we will allow them access to this simple life and watch to see what happens." Later, when the subconscious sees that no damage has been done and it understands the procedure, more important information is released.

The subconscious is not accustomed to being asked for this information, as few people even know it exists. Once access is secured, much more is available through repetition of the procedure and the rapport that is gradually built between subject and director. I believe this rapport is extremely important. If the subconscious suspects any danger or threat to the subject, the information flow would be immediately cut off.

One popular misconception of hypnosis is that it requires the subject to surrender all control. In truth, the subject is in *more* control, not *less* during a hypnotic regression. Even though he appears to be asleep and often does not remember the session upon awakening, the subject is aware of things that are going on in the room that he cannot see or hear through normal means. I have had this demonstrated many times during regressions and believe this is part of the natural monitoring system of the subconscious.

Chapter 2

Life in

Colorado Territory

*B*EFORE I BEGIN AN INDUCTION I like to spend about a half-hour with hypnotic regression subjects. During this time I attempt to find out something about them, answer their questions and allow them to feel more at ease with me. After spending this time with Kathryn, I began the induction.

She slipped quickly and easily into a deep trance. Because of the aforementioned predictability, I was not surprised when Katie began describing a white house, "sitting up there all lonesome," in a countryside of hills and valleys. This was the same type of setting I had heard from many others. When she entered the house, she saw her mother baking bread in an oven in the large kitchen.

K: The kitchen's got a coat room off back. We've got to take our shoes off. And I see the wood stove. Momma's just now taking some things out of the oven.

It was at this point that I noticed a difference between Katie and the other subjects; she could *smell* the bread baking. This is not common and indicated all her senses were being activated. She was also speaking in the first-person, using the word "I." Apparently she was not going to be passive, but an active participate in the regression. Maybe this would not be a run-of-the-mill type, I thought.

Since exact years were difficult to obtain, I usually try to determine what time period we are in by asking for descriptions of clothes, furnishings and surroundings. I asked about her mother.

K: She's got dark hair. I guess some people might think she is a little plump, but I think she is just so. Blue eyes, pretty, and her hair is up. She's got on a blue-flowered cotton that comes to the floor.

I asked her to describe herself. She said her name was Sharon and she was only 12.

K: I have on my yellow dress and my feet are all muddy. (A childish laugh.) Momma will be mad, because I wasn't supposed to go out in my nice dress.
D: *Is there anyone else in your family?*
K: Philip, my brother, and Daddy. Philip's gone to town with Daddy. They went to go get supplies. Daddy had to leave before sunup. It's about a day's drive into town in the wagon. Half a day, anyway.
D: *Do you know the name of the town?*
K: Clear Creek. It's fun to go, except Momma says it's not a good town for girls to go to. It's real wild.
D: *Will they be back in time to eat?*
K: Maybe. Maybe not. Momma will hold dinner for them, though.
D: *Do you like living out in the country?*
K: It's great, you only have to go to school two days a week. I get to running around, Momma says, like a regular hooligan.

When Katie heard the tape played back later, she laughed, saying "hooligan" was not a word she would normally use.

D: *(I laughed.) What grade are you in?*
K: Second.

That was a surprise. Twelve years old and only in the second grade? It appeared she had not attended school as early as we normally do today. And only going two days a week, there was probably not time for her to learn anything but the bare essentials. From my research, I have found that many times girls were not even educated at all.

D: *Do you know how to read and write yet?*

Katie's voice was taking on a different characteristic. It sounded naïve and rather countrified, with a noticeable drawl emerging.

K: Somewhat. I can't see that it's real important though. Don't have to do much figurin' to be a housewife, help take care of the farm.
D: *Is that what you intend on doing when you grow up?*
K: Ain't much else *to* do.

I moved her ahead to dinnertime and asked if the others had returned from town.

K: Yeah, it's late and it's dark outside, but we saved dinner and Paw and Philip are here. They're tired; it's been a long day for them. I wish I could have gone. It's different. It's not like being out here all day.
D: *How often do they go to town?*
K: Twice a month, sometimes. Mostly only once.

I asked what they were having for dinner. From talking to so many people in regressions, I have come to know what time period they are in by the food they eat. I can also tell much from the type of utensils that are used. These are repeated predictable patterns. Many of the questions I ask are used to establish the time frame. It also might be called a test, since the subject does not know what details I am looking for or the pattern that others have supplied.

K: Having stewed chicken, and some of that homemade bread. Some corn on the cob, from our own garden. And some leftover apple pie.
D: *What kind of dishes are you using?*
K: They're blue and white, and they've got pictures on them. They're Momma's pride and joy.

D: *(I knew it was not common to use china.) Does she use them every night?*

K: No, just special. Every other time they're put up in the hutch. Just for lookin' at, stuff like that. (Katie said later she did not know what a hutch was.) Sometimes we use just the wooden bowls. Most times we use stoneware.

I assumed these were settlers and not just people living in the country. The earlier settlers did not have things as nice as this, either in their houses or living conditions. This was more consistent with what I have found from the late 1800s period. So I now knew what time period "Sharon" was probably speaking from.

D: *How old is your brother, Philip?*

K: Sixteen. That's why he gets to go to town, and I have to stay here.

D: *He is becoming a man, that's why.*

K: He's just a mean, old ornery brother. He don't count.

Times have not changed that much. This is still a very common opinion from younger sisters (though it should be noted that in her present life, Katie only has one sister).

D: *(I laughed.) What about your father? Does he look very old?*

K: Oh, he's … I don't know … he is old.

I moved Katie to a time when Sharon was attending school. Even though she didn't think much of it, I thought it would give us an opportunity to find out what a school of that time period was like. I asked for a description.

K: (She spoke with a very heavy drawl.) It is made out of rocks. They said they didn't want no school collapsin' right on kids, so they all pitched in and built it.

This could be another reason for her only being in the second grade. Maybe there hadn't been a school in that area very long.

D: *Is it a very big school?*

K: Naw, only about 12 kids. Some of us are just slower than others. Some of us learn pretty fast. But I don't care.

D: *You don't all learn the same thing then?*

K: No, just sit in the same room.

She had described a typical one-room schoolhouse. I asked about the teacher.

K: She's got blond hair and brown eyes with a kind of mean look on her face. She's not very nice; I don't like her.

D: *Why? Is she real strict?*

K: Yeah! We really get whopped if we don't get into school on time, 'cause she has to stay over. She likes to carry a ruler, and we gets whacked across the knuckles if we don't mind. And that hurts. And she won't let us talk and I don't like that. More fun to get out and run and play.

D: *Okay, Sharon, let's go ahead in your life to some important day.*

This always produces different results, but usually within similar patterns. What we might consider an important day is never what the subject would consider an important day. Their lives in these time periods were so humdrum that any out-of-the-ordinary event was important, making anything likely. This is another example of what I consider proof of reincarnation, because subjects do not invent exciting tales.

I counted Katie forward to an important point in Sharon's life.

K: It's raining. Those people came. (Her voice sounded different— soft and sad.) We buried Papa!

D: *Oh? What happened to him?*

K: (She was almost crying.) He … just died. Doc said his heart stopped.

D: *Where are you?*

K: (Sniffling) I'm … I'm in the graveyard.

D: *How old are you now?*

K: Thirteen.

D: *Is your Mom and Philip there?*

K: Uh-huh. (She sounded very unhappy.)

This was affecting Katie; she was showing genuine emotion. This is another key to the level of the hypnotic state. When subjects feel the events, they are participating, becoming a part of what is happening and are in a lower altered state.

I decided to take her ahead to the age of 14 to remove her from the unhappiness of her father's death. This time I found Sharon out in the field plowing, or "working the plow" as she called it. She said she was helping her momma work the farm, but she didn't like doing that kind of work. They were planting corn and she had a jenny pulling the plow. I asked her what a jenny was.

K: (Slowly, as though she had to think.) A female ... mule.

I wondered why they were doing the work by themselves. She had made no mention of her brother Philip.

D: *Who else lives with you in the house there?*
K: Just me and my maw.
D: *Do you have to take care of that farm by yourself?*
K: Usually. It's hard work, but we get by.
D: *What happened to the men in the family?*
K: My brother, he went away. Couldn't do much. And my daddy died.
D: *Why did your brother leave?*
K: Who knows? (She sighed deeply.) Guess he just didn't like being here. He didn't tell me. He might have told Momma, but she don't talk about it. I think she's hurt.
D: *Has he been gone very long?*
K: No, about six months or so.
D: *That puts a lot of work on your mother and you. What do you think you are going to do? Do you have any plans?*
K: Nuthin' yet. Just stay here and take care of the farm and ... just make do, I guess.
D: *Do you still go to school?*
K: Not any more. We got too much to do around here.

D: *Did you learn very much when you were going to school?*

K: Um, learned how to sign my name, add a little bit, read some. Not much.

I got out a tablet and marker, wondering whether she could sign her name for me. My husband and I had tried this method with startling results in our first adventure into reincarnation which I reported in my book *Five Lives Remembered.*

D: *You said they taught you how to sign your name? Would you do me a favor and sign it for me? I'd sure like to see how you do it.*

Katie opened her eyes and raised up. Leaning on her left elbow, she took the marker in her right hand and wrote the name "Sharon Jackson." It is interesting to note that Katie is normally left-handed, but this personality had no hesitancy about taking the marker in her right hand. Katie's normal handwriting is very small with evenly formed letters. Sharon's writing was large, uneven, uncertain and sprawling, as though she did not have much practice with writing. A handwriting analyst said it bore no resemblance at all to Katie's present handwriting. I complimented Sharon on doing a good job.

K: It's not bad.

D: *Was that hard to learn?*

K: Boring.

D: *Well, at least people can't say you don't know how to write, can they?*

K: Leastwise, I can sign my name.

D: *Can you read very well?*

K: As long as it's printin', not too bad. I can usually figure it out. I just don't know what all the words mean sometimes.

D: *Do you have any books that you can practice with?*

K: Just the Bible. Me and Momma reads it sometimes at nights.

D: *That's one way to learn to read, but it has hard words in it, doesn't it?*

K: Yeah, some of 'em are right strange.

D: *A lot of those words, I don't think anybody knows what they mean.*

K: Some folks just say they do. Make 'em sound more important than others.

D: *But you can read some, and if you can write your name, that is more than a lot of folks can do, isn't it?*

K: Yeah, suppose so.

D: *And you know how to add. You said, to do some numbers?*

K: Yeah. I can figure out enough that they don't cheat me when I go to buy somethin'. I can cipher right good at that.

D: *That's really important to know how to do that. Do you have any boyfriends?*

K: (Shyly) Yeah, sorta.

D: *Anybody in particular?*

K: Naw, not yet.

D: *Well, what kind of things are there to go to around there?*

K: Well, you have dances on Saturday night. People get together ... sometimes have like a barn-raisin' if somebody new moves in. And, folks just use all sorts of excuses to get together and see neighbors they haven't seen for awhile.

D: *That is the social life.*

K: Um-hum, that and church. 'Course there's a lot of church socials.

D: *Everybody comes to all those things?*

K: Naw, not everybody. Some people don't go to church none, so ...

D: *Well, at least you have something to look forward to.*

When I asked her to go ahead to another important day in her life the emotion changed very rapidly and this time she sounded very happy.

K: I'm getting married.

D: *How old are you now?*

K: Sixteen.

D: *What are you doing?*

K: I'm cutting the cake.

D: *Where are you?*

K: At the churchyard. They're having a real regular picnic. The whole town's here.

D: *Did your mother make the cake for you?*

K: Yeah. Momma's a good cook.

D: *Did you learn to cook like her?*

K: Said I don't burn too much anymore, anyway.

D: *Who are you marrying?*

K: His name's Tom, Tom Jacobs. Oh, he's handsome. Got real dark hair and green eyes.

D: *How old is he?*

K: Twenty-six.

D: *Oh, he's older than you.*

K: Cause ... like Momma said, he's made his mark.

D: *What does that mean?*

K: He spent all his young years learning how to make a trade, and doing things. So now he's ready to settle down. He's a blacksmith. Makes good money.

D: *What kind of dress do you have on?*

K: Blue. (I was a little surprised the dress wasn't white.) It's silk! It's got a white row collar, and real puffed sleeves. It even has a little train that Momma fixed up for in back.

D: *Did your Momma make the dress?*

K: Nooo! She just made the train. She actually bought a store-bought dress. Something special.

Maybe this was why it was not white; just being a store-bought dress would have been special enough. It is also possible that white dresses were harder to find. They surely would not have been very practical.

D: *Do you have anything on your head?*

K: Got Momma's veil.

D: *Is your Momma happy?*

K: Yeah. She thinks I done real well for myself.

D: *Where are you going to live with Tom?*

K: In his house, behind the blacksmith shop. He's got a real nice place fixed up. It's big enough for the two of us, and ... one more, maybe. Probably won't stay there long. Not if we decide to start a family.

D: *Are you planning on starting a family?*

K: (Shyly) Yeah. I like having kids.

D: *Well, where is the blacksmith shop—in the main part of town?*

K: Out towards the edge. But it's still in the nice part of town. You get plenty of business. He does real good work.

D: *Are there any other stores right around where the shop is?*

K: Yeah, there's a hardware store. And then there's a general mercantile down the way. (Katie had never heard the word "mercantile.") And we've got the telegraph office next door to it.

D: *Then you won't have to go very far to get anything you need. Is there a newspaper in town?*

K: The *Gazette*.

D: *Is that the only name for the paper?*

K: That's all anybody ever called it.

D: *You said the name of the town was Clear Creek? What state are you living in?*

K: Oh, we ain't a state yet. We're just a territory. Called … Territory of … umm, Colorado.

D: *Do you think someday it might be a state?*

K: They're having an awful big argument about that. Of course I don't see what it matters much whether we're a state or just a territory. Don't matter much to me. You work the same anyway. But the men argue. They get silly of it sometimes. Sometimes they get out and have regular fist fights over it.

D: *Oh? Why wouldn't they want to be a state?*

K: Some people says, why should we pay taxes to somebody that's all the way across the country. Other people say that being a state's a great thing. I like to keep out of arguments like that.

D: *Oh, you know how men are.*

K: Yeah, they're all ornery and bull-headed.

D: *All the arguing probably won't have anything to do with it anyway. Okay, this has been a happy day. Let's move ahead to another important day in your life.*

This has proven to be an effective way to move the story forward without leading or influencing the subject. It allows them to tell their own story in their own way while I just follow along and guide them through it. If I did not move them, they might spend the entire session describing all the details of one scene.

K: I just had Jamie. He's so sweet.

D: *What, did you have a baby?*

K: Uh-huh. My first one; it's a little boy. He's sweet. He's so tiny.

D: *Where was he born?*

K: At home.

D: *Is anybody with you?*

K: Momma.

D: *Where's Tom?*

K: He had to leave. Said that he'd be back. He ain't made it back yet.

D: *Where did he have to go?*

K: To Denver.

D: *Is that very far?*

K: It's a long ways. Couple of hundred miles. He rode, sending a delegation to Denver.

D: *Is that why he had to go?*

K: Yes. He's real important now.

D: *What's the delegation for?*

K: Some of the arguments as to whether or not we're gonna … Some people wantin' to be a state. He decided he's for it. They're talkin' about makin' what they call a … Constitution? Something like that. I don't pay much attention. But he thinks it's important.

D: *That's an honor for them to pick him to go.*

K: Because he's real smart.

D: *Did they all ride together?*

K: Yeah. Took a couple of wagons, but most of them rode on horseback.

D: *How do you feel about him not being there?*

K: I'm sad. Wish he was here to see Jamie. He decided that we would name him Jamie if it was a boy.

D: *How old are you now?*

K: Eighteen.

D: *Let's go forward a little bit until Tom has come back. What does he think of the new baby?*

K: He thinks he's special. He thinks he's cute.

D: *How did he feel about not being there?*

K: He was upset. But he'll get over it, and there'll be others.

D: *What did the delegation decide?*

K: They had a bunch of arguments, but they finally got it smoothed out, and they decided they want to become a state. They're gonna go ahead and do it.

D: *It's complicated, but Tom understands it, doesn't he?*

K: Because he's smart.

D: *Well, it sounds like you are having a happy life. You are 18? Let's go forward to when you are about 25 and see what is happening in your life at that time.*

I decided to direct her because she was only moving ahead a few years at a time and at this rate it could take quite a while to get the story of her life. Thus far her important days were very common. The only unusual thing was her telling of the delegation and arguments surrounding Colorado becoming a state. If someone were inventing a story, these are details that they would not include. Their presence adds validity to any account.

D: *I will count to three. One, two, three. You are 25 years old. What is happening?*

K: Nothing. I'm not there!

This response was a surprise, but when it happens it always means the personality died sometime before that age. It also is further proof that I am not leading the subject. If Katie was merely creating a story to please me, why didn't she continue since I directed her to go to a specific age?

When this occurs, I always return the subject to the last scene they witnessed as that personality and pick it up from that point to determine what happened.

D: *Okay. Let's go back to when you were 18 and you just had the baby. And Tom had just come back from Denver. Can you find that girl for me again?*

K: Yes.

D: *Okay, let's take her forward. Does she ever have any more children?*

K: One. A girl. They called her Jennie.

D: *Jennie? Okay, how old are you when you have Jennie?*
K: Nineteen. (She frowned.)
D: *What's wrong?*
K: It's real bad. She came backward.

I gave her reassuring suggestions that she would not be physically affected. Occasionally with deep trance subjects, the body will also remember the event and produce very real physical reactions.

K: Something's wrong. I ... I don't know. I'm ... just not there.
D: *You mean you're watching it?*
K: Yeah.

This meant that she was not in the body and therefore could not feel anything, so we could explore the situation with no discomfort to Katie.

D: *What do you see? Was there anything wrong with the baby?*
K: She started to strangle. But, Doc says there is complications.
D: *You had a doctor this time?*
K: Yes. Momma's real upset; she's crying. She wanted it to be fast.
D: *What are the complications? (No answer) What happened to Sharon?*
K: (Very sadly) She died.
D: *Couldn't the doctor do anything?*
K: No. Lost a lot of blood. It was too much.
D: *Was Tom there this time?*
K: Yeah, but he couldn't help either. He got so upset. ... Momma's cryin'.
D: *Well, what did they do with Sharon's body?*

I always ask this because people usually wonder about what happened to their body.

K: They buried her up on the hill. (She sounded so sad.)
D: *What are you going to do now?*
K: Go back home.

D: *Where is home?*
K: (A long pause) I don't know.

The voice of Sharon that came from Katie was not similar to her normal voice. It was childish in the beginning, naïve and countrified later, and had a very innocent quality and noticeable drawl throughout.

After I reassured her, and gave her suggestions for well-being, I brought Katie forward to the present time and awakened her. She said she had no memory of the session except that it had something to do with Colorado.

When I began research into Colorado history I could find no mention of a town called Clear Creek, but a creek by that name and Clear Creek County have a firm place in early Colorado history. The gold rush began in that area and it was the heart of early development. Around 1861 mining camps sprang up all over the area and millions in gold was taken out of the mountains. By 1870 Clear Creek County was one of the leading producers of precious metals in Colorado. Many of these mining camps developed into towns while others did not flourish. It was a wild and boisterous area with few laws during that time, so it fits the description Sharon gave.

However, the area is not located a couple of hundred miles from Denver, as Sharon said. It actually is about 35 miles west of Denver. But I suspect even that would seem a long way to a barely educated, naïve girl who had never been very far from home. Especially when her husband left while she was expecting her first baby any day. It might just as well have been a couple of hundred miles.

Throughout the 1860s groups of delegates met in Denver several times to agree on a constitution for the territory and to decide the fixing of boundaries. At each of these conventions the question of Colorado becoming a state was raised. Each time their efforts were defeated by the voters. Open resistance developed over the matter of tax collection. The people, especially in the mountain districts, threatened to arm themselves against any tax officers who would attempt to enforce any tax laws.

Colorado did not become a state until 1876 mainly because of this outspoken hostility. Conventions were constantly being held up until that time, so Tom Jacobs could have attended any one of these.

I am inclined to think that Sharon lived in the Clear Creek area during the 1860s and early 1870s because settlers did not descend on Colorado until after the gold rush began. And their living conditions seemed to be too nice and the town sounded too developed to have been one of the first settlements.

As I had suspected, Katie was proving to be no ordinary subject. She went deep quickly, demonstrated sensory sensations, experienced emotion and remembered virtually nothing upon awakening. Katie was a true somnambulist. This is a person who is capable of reaching the deepest trance state, and in regression, will completely become the other personality. Dick Sutphen, noted reincarnation expert, says that only one out of ten people can achieve this level. I knew that this was the best type of subject for my type of research and I eagerly wanted to continue working with Katie if she was willing.

Chapter 3

The Resting Lives

WE HAD MADE THE INITIAL BREAKTHROUGH and discovered what an excellent somnambulistic subject Katie was. She was a little overwhelmed and had her doubts about where the story had come from. She asked me how I could tell if a memory was real. How did I know it was not just her wild imagination?

I explained that if the subject expressed true emotion the information was believable because this cannot be faked under hypnosis. Sharon had expressed true sadness at the death of her father in Colorado and grief when she died so young in childbirth. She felt a reluctance to leave her husband and the life there. When such true human feelings are expressed, you know you have hit home. You have uncovered something deep inside that was waiting to come out.

Upon awakening the subject is often embarrassed. Their conscious mind tells them they were being silly because these events had nothing to do with them. This is the so-called "logic" of the conscious mind. It tries to explain away something it does not want to understand by saying, in effect, "You probably read this somewhere or saw it in a movie or on television." Upon reflection, the subject will usually realize that the events were felt too deeply and seemed too real to be imaginary. Emotions are the key.

With that explanation, Katie said simply, "Good, that's all I wanted to know. You've answered my question ... something I've been wondering about. I don't want to talk about it now ... maybe someday." She did not explain further, but there was something different about her expression. Her normally carefree attitude vanished and she grew serious and seemed lost in thought. I had a feeling there was something bothering her that had no connection with the Colorado life, but I did not know her well enough at the time to question her about it. I told her any time she was ready we could talk about it.

During the next session, I conditioned Katie to go into a deep somnambulistic trance with a keyword. This is done often for the convenience of the guide (myself), so a longer induction is not necessary. When a subject has been conditioned in this way, the hypnotist has only to mention the keyword (which can be anything) and the subject will go immediately into the deep trance state.

I always add the suggestion that the individual will only go if they are willing. This way the subject knows he is still in control and does not have to be afraid I might try to put him under at an inconvenient time or against his will. This technique has proven very useful in building rapport, since subjects realize they do not have to fear me and know I will only work in cooperation with them. It is important to help dispel the popular image of the stage hypnotist, who makes people perform all sorts of embarrassing acts with the snap of his fingers.

As Katie and I worked together the next few weeks, I allowed her subconscious to pick and choose which lives we would explore. I was not as yet directing her to go anywhere, and we uncovered a few insignificant *resting lives.*

A resting life can be defined as an insignificant life, although I do not think any life is truly insignificant. Each life is the unique story of a human being and, as such, all have merit. A resting life can be long or short. It is one where the entity appears to coast through a dull, seemingly meaningless life where nothing really extraordinary happens.

We all know people like this, who seem to skate through life with nothing bothering them. They do not make waves. Karma may be repaid and worked out in such a life, however, apparently without creating new karma. I imagine everyone needs a life like this once in a while as we could not continually go from one traumatic life to another without relaxing.

The resting life is perfect for this and thus it has merit, even though the personality might seem dull and unimportant. This may also help us to understand people in our own life experiences who are living this type of life now. We should realize that we cannot judge, without knowing what type of life the person is resting from, what their accomplishments may have been before and what they may accomplish the next time around.

As I have said, this is often the type of life the subconscious picks for viewing when a subject first begins to experiment with regression. The life of Sharon in Colorado is typical. When these are chosen, I always know there was some pretty heavy trauma in the past that is being temporarily hidden. The purpose of my guidance is to build rapport with the subject's subconscious so that these more significant lives can also be revealed when the personality feels ready to deal with them. The following are three such lives that were encountered during this beginning trial period.

One was Joshua, a young orphan we found living in the woods. He was only 12 but had become quite capable of taking care of himself. He had to, he said, because there was nobody else to trust.

D: *What happened to your mother and father?*
K: Mom died. She got killed by the soldiers. I never knew my father.

The accent was decidedly English. The voice was very soft. I got the impression that Joshua was not used to talking to people. His answers were slow, as though he had to think before answering.

D: *Why did they kill her?*
K: Why do soldiers do anything? They wanted the town. There was fighting in the area. Who knows over what? It didn't matter. The soldiers came in the middle of the town. They burned the town, left me for dead. (The voice was very quiet, shy and childlike.)
D: *If you had stayed in the town, wouldn't you have been all right?*
K: It killed her! They'd probably killed me, too!
D: *Are you very far from the village?*
K: Maybe half a day.
D: *What do you do when you get hungry?*
K: Go out and trap a rabbit with my snare, or maybe even a pig, steal a chicken and roast it. Sometimes I just eat berries if they are in

season. When it gets cold, things are hard to find, but in the springtime it's not too bad.

D: *Where do you sleep?*

K: Sometimes I make me a lean-to of trees. Sometimes just out under the stars if it ain't rainin'.

D: *What do you do for clothes?*

K: Skin the animals I catch, tan the hides.

D: *Umm, that's a little odd to live like that.*

K: Maybe some folks think so. I can take care of myself. Don't have to worry about anybody but myself.

D: *Does it ever bother you, being alone?*

K: No, I'm never alone. I talk to the animals and the birds and at least they don't argue with me. I have a lot to keep me busy. People are a bother.

D: *Do you have a last name, Joshua?*

K: Only rich people have last names.

D: *Why are you living in the woods?*

K: It's not safe to venture out on your own. Not in open country. Sheriff's men might get you. They're always needing slaves. Vals.

D: *Why would they want to catch you if you are not bothering anyone?*

K: You call poaching King's deer not bothering anybody? They kill men for less. Seen a man hung for it.

D: *Do you think the sheriff knows you are out there?*

K: Naw, I'm careful.

D: *Where do the other people live?*

K: Mostly in town. Around the forts. I don't go there; people aren't much good.

I knew I was going to have a little more difficulty trying to establish the time frame and country if the boy was living like a hermit in the woods. He said it was Brittany, but it sounded like it might be England, with the mention of the King's deer, the Sheriff and the slaves. I wondered if these things existed in other countries besides England? I had to try to think of questions that might help to determine the time frame.

D: *Did you ever hear anybody say what year it was?*

K: (Pause, then as though reciting.) The year of our Lord ... eleven
     ... six ... six.

I was glad to get that because the year is the hardest thing to obtain
in regressions.

D: *What do the other people look like? Do you ever see them?*
K: Yeah, sometimes I see them from a distance. The women wear
     long dresses, out of wool, I guess. The men wear jerkins and
     breech cloaks (unclear) and britches.

Research disclosed that a jerkin was a small vestlike jacket usually
made of leather. Maybe a breech cloak was a short cloak that only
reached the breeches (another name for britches). These clothes were
consistent with the 12th and 13th centuries.

D: *Do they have anything on their heads?*
K: Some of them do. Some of them have hats. Some of 'em wear
     capes with hoods.
D: *Do the women have anything on their heads?*
K: Rich ones. Rich ones wear nets. (I didn't understand.) Nets!
     Cauls.

I wasn't sure of what Joshua meant at the time, but I later found
it was correct, according to clothing styles of that period. The richer
women did wear nets over the back of their hair.
     I decided to move Joshua ahead to an important day in his life,
although I could not imagine what would be important to someone
living in the woods all alone. One day must have been just like
another. I counted him ahead and asked what he was doing. He was
hiding up in a tree watching a procession going through the woods.

K: It's like there's rich, fancy people, all dressed up. A lot of soldiers.
     Got to make sure nobody sees me.
D: *Yes, you have to be careful. Is it only soldiers?*
K: No, there's a ... funny-looking box. It's got a horse pullin' it, and
     one on the other end. (I thought he meant a carriage.) It's got a

lady in it. It's got curtains. And she had it all pulled shut so she could stick her head out. There's a couple of men in fancy dress. Got on really soft-looking capes and big pins holding 'em. Lots of jewelry.

D: *It sounds like they must be rich.*

K: Have to be to have that many soldiers.

D: *Do the fancy-dressed men have any hats on?*

K: No. One's got a silver thing around his head, that's all.

He said they were clean-shaven. I asked how the soldiers were dressed, still believing you can learn much about time periods from the clothing.

K: Got heavy … chain … chain coats. They've got helmets, rounded, kinda, with a thing that comes over their nose and the side of their face. Great big, long swords.

Joshua had no idea who these people were or where they were going. It was just a very unusual occurrence to have anyone come through his portion of the woods.

K: Probably somebody marrying her. Want to make sure she gets there. She don't look very happy. Somebody says … Winifred … Swanson? Something like that.

D: *Are they talking to each other?*

K: Yeah. You can just barely hear 'em.

D: *Is there anyone inside the box with her?*

K: Can't tell. You can just see her, she sticks her head out.

D: *Where do you think they are going to?*

K: I don't know, maybe a castle. There is one aways away. Who knows?

I asked for a better description of the box-like thing the lady was riding in.

K: Got a real strong-lookin' roof, kinda round posts on the edge. It's got sides with a window on each side. And it's suspended on posts between horses, one in front and one in back.

D: *(I still thought Joshua was talking about a regular carriage.) How*
    many horses are pulling it?
K: Just the one in front and the one in back. They've got on harness.

It is always strange to me what someone sees as an important day.
When it is something like this, it is proof that the subject is not fantasizing because it is not something dramatic. I took Katie ahead again
to another important day in Joshua's life and she started breathing
heavily and became disturbed.

K: Can't see! It hurts!

This was sudden but I gave Katie reassuring suggestions that she
would not really feel any physical sensations. She could remove herself from that part of it, if she wished, so she could tell me objectively
what had happened.

K: (She was still breathing heavily.) Been shot! They caught me! A
    soldier caught me ... catching a deer. ... They shot me!
D: *What was wrong about catching a deer?*
K: For the King ... nobleman. I had no right.

Joshua was only 15 when this happened and had apparently spent
most of his life in the woods living by his wits—a perfect example of
a resting life. There was so little diversion in his life that he had
difficulty finding any important days for me.
    One interesting thing was his description of the box-like vehicle.
I naturally thought it was a carriage, until I began to do research.
Carriages as we know them did not come along until much later,
mainly because of the slow development of roads. This was a surprise
to me because we so often see carriages in movies based on this time
period.
    I found that the vehicle described was a litter, something I do not
remember ever seeing in movies of these time periods. The pictures
of a litter look very similar to Joshua's description of a box-like
structure covered with curtains and without wheels. It had posts on
the corners and was supported on two long poles that were attached

to two horses, one in front and one in back, with riders on the horses to direct them. I have been told these are not seen in movies or TV because it is difficult to train the horse in back to follow such a contraption, as it cannot see where it is going.

A quote from *Colliers' Encyclopedia* on the litter: "During the Middle Ages the roads in Europe were few and muddy, so that horseback or muleback was the usual mode of transportation. This method of travel was difficult for the old and ill and was thought to be beneath the dignity of a woman of rank. Consequently, the litter, a couch with an enclosed superstructure, which protected the passenger from rain and wind, was widely used by travelers who could afford the luxury. Such litters, supported by horses or mules, were used in Europe from the 11th into the 17th century."

This would have been considered a simple regression with nothing of importance in it, if not for the mention of the litter. This showed that Katie was not relying on information stored in her conscious mind from movies and TV programs.

Though this was my first encounter with a litter, it was not to be my last. It popped up many times as I worked with various people. It must have been a popular means of transportation during that time period. I also have never yet had a subject slip up and put a carriage into the wrong time slot, which should prove something in relation to reincarnation regressive experiments.

A SIMILAR EXAMPLE of a resting life occurred a week later, when the following personality emerged with a very soft voice that was difficult to hear at times. The speech was also very slow. This was someone who was not used to being rushed.

K: I see forests ... great huge trees. ... It is raining.
D: *Where are you? Do you know?*
K: I am in my home, my land. (Pause) The land does not have a name, it is just the land.

This has occurred many times when I encounter primitive personalities. They frequently call the place they live "the land" and they are merely "the people."

D: *What are you doing?*
K: We are hunting.
D: *Who is "we"? Are there others with you?*
K: There's my brother, yes.
D: *What are you hunting for?*
K: We are hunting for food. Maybe monkey.
D: *Do you have any kind of weapons?*
K: I use my dart gun, or sometimes I build traps … to spring. We have our blowguns. And we have bows and arrow.

The entity identified itself as a male named Tocoricam (phonetic spelling). I asked how he was dressed.

K: I have my … breechcloth (as if difficult to find the right word) and my shoes. They are made out of leather and … sewn together.

This personality seemed to be searching to find the correct words. I don't believe he had words in his vocabulary to answer some of my questions.

D: *Doesn't it get cold wearing so few clothes?*
K: It is always hot.

This is rather like detective work, tracking down all the clues available. Still trying to determine what type of native this was, I asked about the color of his skin. He said it was "kind of a reddish-brown, the color of the soil." His hair was black. I thought this would probably eliminate those living in the jungles of the African continent. He also said he was about 20 summers old.

D: *Do you live near here?*
K: We live a ways down the river, yes.

I can always get more information from the type of living conditions, so I counted him to the place where he lived and asked him to describe it for me. I naturally expected a hut in a village, assuming this would have been a normal response.

K: It is … we have holed out the side of the cliff and made a very small cave. It is just enough to keep us out of the rain. And there is a fire. And there are mats where everyone sleeps at the back. (This was an unexpected answer.)

D: *Are there many in your family?*

K: There are only about five of us. There is my brother and myself. There is my sister and my two parents … my mother and my father.

D: *Then you hunt for the food to feed your family?*

K: Yes, one must eat to survive, and we find roots and we … it is good.

D: *Are there other families besides yours?*

K: Yes, there are many who have hidden. Sometimes we find others, but mostly we stay to ourselves.

D: *Do you grow anything?*

K: No. To grow one must stay in one place. And to stay in one place means to be found. We live off the land. There is plenty here for us, for those who know how to live. We must always move. It is not safe. The strange ones come and they look for people to take. And we must hide.

D: *You called them the "strange ones." Why do you call them that?*

K: They ride on great beasts and they kill other people like it was … they were nothing to them. They are not from the land.

D: *You mean they have come from somewhere outside? Are they different from your people?*

K: Yes, they are … their skin is light compared to us. And they are very angry men. They have … great things that … (having difficulty again with description) uh, spit smoke and men fall. It is not good.

Apparently this was the first time he had seen a gun in use.

D: *You said they ride on great beasts? What do the beasts look like?*

K: They are almost as tall as a man, and they have four legs. And pointed ears. And a great long, thick neck, and a large head with big rolling eyes.

This is an excellent description of a horse by someone who had never seen one. In mentioning the big rolling eyes, it became obvious that he must have been terrified by this strange prancing creature.

D: *You have never seen an animal like that before?*
K: No. They are not from here.
D: *You said these strange ones ride on these beasts and they come into the forest and take people? Do you know where they take them?*
K: Yes, they want people to work in their mines. People die there; it is not a good place.
D: *What kind of mines do they have?*
K: They take stones out of the ground. Who knows why they want it? The land does not like this.
D: *Are the mines near where you live?*
K: No, they are over the mountain range.

As always, I adjusted my questions and attitude to fit the type of personality I am speaking to.

D: *Then, to go there would be to go away from your land, wouldn't it?*
K: Yes, and to go into danger. We will stay in ... here, where it is ... comparatively safe. We did not always live like this. They raided the villages when I was young. They came, and they herded people like animals and took them away.
D: *Does your tribe have a name?*
K: We are just called the people ... The people are one with the land and the land cries out.
D: *That's why you must keep moving, so they won't find you. Do they come into the forest very often?*
K: Usually they stay ... fairly close, but sometimes they have ... people they will go in bunches and they will make raids. Who knows why they do it?

This was interesting, but it was not really telling me much about where he was. I moved him ahead to an important day in his life, although I thought there would be little likelihood of anything unusual happening unless he was captured by these "strange ones."

K: I'm in my canoe. I go down river. (His voice was slow and deliberate with an odd accent.) The forest is very thick. It grows to the very edge of the river. There are many animals and ... the sky is very blue.

D: *Where did you get the canoe?*

K: We built it. We took a log that had fallen and ... hollowed it out.

D: *Was it hard to do?*

K: Just time consuming.

D: *Did you have tools to make it with?*

K: Stones that were sharp. It would take the wood that was dried out.

D: *It must have taken a long time to make.*

K: Several days.

D: *Where are you going in your canoe?*

K: We go to a place that is safer. Where the strange ones do not come. We want to just be alone. To not have to worry about being taken. The strange ones, they come and they take our people to the great holes in the ground to work, and they are never seen again.

D: *Where do the strange ones come from? Do you know?*

K: They come from out of the jungle riding great beasts. I do not know ... We go to a place where they will not find us.

D: *Will it take long to find a place like that, where you will be safe?*

K: Who knows when we will see someplace that may be able to give us life. We will know.

I left him to go down the river looking for safety and moved Katie ahead to another important day in that life.

K: (Sigh) I am watching the body. It shakes. It has the fever ... and it is dying.

D: *Where is the body?*

K: It is along the river. We had made camp there, and ... the fever came. It is something that ... if one of the people would get the fever, sometimes the bark would help. But there is none of the tree ... so I am dying. My father, he is not a medicine man. He does not have all of the knowledge. (Sigh) He is sad.

D: *If you could find that one tree it might help?*

K: Then it is not always sure. Just sometimes. It is the god's will.
D: *Were you very old when you died that way?*
K: I had, maybe, 21, 22 summers. My time had come.
D: *Did the strange ones ever find your people, your family?*
K: Not while I was there. They hid.

This was another good example of a resting life. The entity did not create any further karma and lived a very uneventful life. Again, this would have been a simple regression except for the description of the horse and the strange ones. These are details that would not be provided if someone were trying to fantasize. In a fantasy a great deal more would have occurred. And this was surely fertile material from which to concoct an adventure, if that had been the intention.

There was a few clues in this regression that helped me to locate the setting and the date. I assumed it was somewhere in the jungles of South America. The bark referred to was probably quinine, which comes from the Cinchona tree. These are native to the Andes, from Colombia to Peru, and are used as a cure for malaria, the "fever" from which he undoubtedly died.

Spanish colonization of South America began in the last half of the 1500s. Hungry for wealth, they began mining for emeralds and precious metals. Research revealed that the native South American Indians were cruelly exploited during this era and were put to work in the mines under extremely harsh conditions. In later sessions, whenever I took Katie to the year 1650, I would find this native. This was consistent with the Spanish colonial period.

𝒜NOTHER RESTING LIFE that came through in those early weeks was Gretchen, a five year old child with long blond braids.

D: *What do you see?*
K: I see a castle on the hill. It has big, tall points on each corner, and it is made of gray stone. And the grounds, it's kind of fenced around. It's very big. (Katie was now speaking with a definite German accent which made some words hard to understand.)
D: *Where are you?*

K: Down in the forest.
D: *Are there any people around?*
K: My father is over there cutting wood.
D: *What are you doing?*
K: Picking flowers.
D: *Do you live in the castle?*
K: Nein. I live in a cottage.
D: *What is your father going to do with the wood that he cuts?*
K: He will sell it in the town. It's not really a town, it's just a village.

She said they were not far from the town, but it did not have a name that she could think of. I asked her if the castle had a name.

K: Braunfit. (Phonetically: Brauns-fight.)
D: *Do you know who lives in the castle?*
K: The Duke. (When asked his name she couldn't come up with it.)
D: *Is your father the only one in the family?*
K: Oh, nein. There is my brother, Hans. Just Hans and me … and father.
D: *What happened to your mother?*
K: She died when I was a baby. Cholera.

When I asked for her father's name, she responded "Wilhelm" with the correct German pronunciation. I moved her to the place where she lived to get a description of it.

K: The walls are white, with a great big open fireplace with a sort of arch. And it only has two rooms, the front room and one bedroom.
D: *Do you all sleep in the same room?*
K: All except father, he sleeps in the front.
D: *Is there any furniture in the front room?*
K: The great big bed. And a couple of chairs and a table.
D: *It doesn't seem like a very big house.*
K: Oh, nein. But it is big enough.
D: *Who does the cooking?*
K: Me and Hans. There's an arm that swings over the fireplace that

we hang pots from. And if we are cooking meat, we have a spit to
put it on. Everyone must help. If we don't work, we don't eat.

This sounded very familiar. It was the same terminology the other
German girl used in my first book, *Five Lives Remembered.*

K: Sometimes, if father makes enough from the wood, then we have
     brown bread; sometimes he buys a hog. Sometimes he hunts in
     the forest and we have fresh meat. Sometimes deer, sometimes
     wild boar.
D: *What does he use to kill the animals he hunts?*
K: His bow and arrow.

As always, I asked a test question to eliminate the remote possibility of fantasizing.

D: *What do you do in the wintertime when food isn't growing?*
K: Use potatoes, and hope we catch some rabbits in the traps.
D: *You don't go hungry, do you?*
K: Oh, nein. And we stay warm.
D: *What kind of clothes do you have on, Gretchen?*
K: Today I have on my red dirndl, with a white blouse with flowers
     all over it.

I had never heard of a dirndl before, until I began my research. It
was described as a wide skirt with a colored or white apron and a tight-
fitting bodice. The outfit is worn with a white blouse or a scarf, which
is tucked into the bodice. It is the national dress of the Bavarian and
Austrian Alps.

D: *What kind of shoes do you have?*
K: Wooden ones.

This was a surprise, but I remembered that Holland was not the
only place where wooden shoes were worn.

D: *Aren't they hard to wear?*

K: To keep the feet warm, we stuff them with straw.
D: *It seems like they would be hard to walk in.*
K: You learn.

I thought she was probably too young to tell me much more, so I moved her to an important day when she was older.

K: We're going to the castle.
D: *How old are you now?*
K: Ten.
D: *Why are you going to the castle?*
K: My father wants to see if we can find work there.
D: *Isn't he still cutting wood?*
K: Ja, but growing mouths take more food.
D: *What type of work is he looking for?*
K: He wants to maybe work in the stables. And maybe I can work in the kitchen. I think I would like that.
D: *What about Hans? Is he going too?*
K: (The mention of her brother seemed to make her sad.) Hans left. They took him in the army. There is a war. There is always war.
D: *Who took him?*
K: The Duke's men. (She sounded sad.)
D: *Do you ever hear from him?*
K: Nein.
D: *(I decided to get back to the subject at hand.) Have you ever been in the castle before?*
K: (In awe) Oh, nein.
D: *This would be an experience then, wouldn't it? What are you doing now?*
K: I'm down in the kitchen. It's big.
D: *Will you be the only one working there?*
K: Oh, nein. There are ten other kitchen maids. And four cooks.
D: *That's a lot. Do you have to cook for many people?*
K: I don't cook, I'm not up to that. I just scrub pots.
D: *Do you think you'll ever get to see any other part of the castle?*
K: Maybe if I'm lucky enough to serve, yes.
D: *Are you going to stay at the castle or are you going to go back to your house?*

K: Oh, nein, it's too far. We'll stay at the castle. They have a room above the kitchen where they let me sleep.
D: *Do you share it with anyone else?*
K: Ja, all the kitchen maids.
D: *Where will your father sleep?*
K: In the stables.
D: *There must be a lot of horses.*
K: Oh, ja. Always in and out.

She was saying that he would receive money for his work, but she would not, when suddenly she seemed uncomfortable. When I asked what was wrong, she said, "It's so cold!" and began to cough. This was a surprise.

D: *Where is it cold? In the kitchen or where you sleep?*
K: Nein. (Her voice sounded as if she was shivering.)
D: *Where are you?*
K: (Still shivering.) Lost! (I was confused.) It's snowing. (She started coughing again.)

This was a typical example of the instability that subjects often experience when they first begin working with regression. They have a tendency to skip around both forward and backward within the time frame and sometimes even jump out of the time frame altogether into an entirely different life. This happens spontaneously, without direction. When the subconscious becomes more accustomed to working with regression, such jumps usually stop and the subject can stabilize, holding the scene.

Because Katie was experiencing physical symptoms, I gave her suggestions of well-being to relieve any discomfort, and asked how she got out in the snow.

K: We were going back to the cottage.
D: *Why? I thought you were going to work at the castle?*
K: Because we wanted to get some of our things, and the snow came up.
D: *Is it snowing very much?*

K: You can't see.

D: *Oh, that's why you're lost. Is your father with you?*

K: Yes, he's so tired.

D: *Do you have far to go?*

K: Who knows? We could be walking around in circles.

D: *Is it dark or daytime?*

K: I guess it is still a little daylight, the clouds are so thick though. Through the trees, we cannot see.

D: *Then you could be going in circles. What are you going to do?*

K: (Frightened) I don't know.

D: *All right, what do you do?*

I counted to three and told her she would know what happened and it wouldn't bother her to talk about it.

K: (Pause) We tried to build a fire.

D: *Could you find any dry wood?*

K: (Sadly) Nein, none of it would burn.

D: *Then what happened?*

K: First came the wolf ... from out of the woods ... he attacked my father.

D: *Why do you think it attacked him?*

K: Why do wolves attack? They are always hungry.

D: *Did your father have any kind of weapon?*

K: Just his stick. He tried to beat it off, but it was too strong for him ... It killed him!

D: *What did you do then?*

K: I tried to climb the tree, but it didn't do any good.

D: *What happened?*

K: I left the body. The wolf killed me.

D: *The same wolf?*

K: One of them.

D: *How old were you, Gretchen, when this happened?*

K: Eleven.

This showed she had jumped ahead a year without being told to do so. She was ten when she first went to the castle to work and then, suddenly, she was on the day of her death a year later.

I gave Katie instructions and reassurances before I awakened her. In later sessions, while going backward through time in a more orderly sequence, we again encountered Gretchen in the same scene where she was lost in the woods. It again made her shiver and caused her distress to be cold and lost.

I thought Gretchen's life was in Germany, until the dirndl was mentioned. That narrowed it down to Bavaria or Austria. This lifetime would have been difficult to date except for the mention of her mother dying from cholera. This puzzled me because I knew cholera was an Asiatic disease.

Research disclosed that cholera spread to Europe, appearing there first in 1830, again in 1848 and followed with a terrible epidemic in 1854. Any of these dates would have placed this life immediately preceding the life of Sharon in Colorado, who also had a short, uneventful life. There were duchies—territories ruled by dukes—in Bavaria, and both Austria and Bavaria experienced short wars during this time period and had to raise armies several times.

In all, during a year's work, I uncovered 26 of Katie's lives, which contained a wealth of information concerning a wide variety of cultures and religious beliefs. These will be put in order in another book and the interrelating patterns of karma will be traced.

For now, her subconscious was still playing games, refusing to delve deeper into lives that would have significance for her.

All during these weeks that we worked together, I had the feeling there was something else, just beneath the surface, that Katie was reluctant to talk to me about—something of importance to her.

Chapter 4

The Secret
Is Revealed

KATIE WAS BEGINNING TO ADJUST to the idea of reincarnation and the possibility that these lives she was reliving while in trance could possibly have been real. Otherwise, where could they be coming from? Even in these apparently simple lives there were historical and geographical details that she was not familiar with due to her limited schooling. If she was going to fantasize, surely she would have brought up "safe" areas, things she knew about from movies, books or TV.

She was also becoming accustomed to me and we were building a good working relationship. One afternoon, as we sat talking about the day's session, she confirmed my suspicions that there was something else lying just beneath the surface. She decided to tell me what had been bothering her.

Katie had been mulling over what I had told her about the emotions being the key to a genuine memory. She thought that might be the explanation for a curious event that had happened about six months before I met her, an event that had caused her great emotion and trauma. She had felt it was too strange to tell anyone and had held it secretly inside of her. If it didn't make sense to *her*, how could she expect it to make sense to anyone else.

So, afraid of being ridiculed or being considered crazy by so-called "rational" people, she had kept it to herself. But it was still bothering her and she decided to risk ridicule as she announced, "What would you say if I told you that I think I may have died in an atomic bomb explosion in Japan?"

What would I say? I was startled, but because I believe in reincarnation I knew it was possible. From the standpoint of a writer, I thought it would be an interesting avenue to explore.

I'm sure everyone knows that when the first atomic bomb was dropped on Hiroshima it was a major event that brought about the end of World War II and ushered in the Atomic Age. As I am always interested in exploring the events of history firsthand with this method of regressive hypnosis, this presented a fascinating challenge. I also keep looking for recent historical events that would be easier to research, so of course I was interested in the possibility. But at that time, Katie did not want to check it out through regression, the feelings were too intense. She had begun to feel comfortable with me and just wanted to talk about it.

"I know it sounds crazy, but I remember being there!" she sighed heavily. "And I don't understand it."

Going on the assumption that someday we might be able to uncover more about this, I wanted to know Katie's conscious memories before they could possibly be colored by hypnotic recall. I urged her to tell me about the day the memory first emerged.

She said she was home alone at the time. Not having much to do, she turned on the TV. There was a documentary-type show on, where an interviewer was questioning a Japanese woman. She never did catch the name of the program, but she idly listened to what they were talking about. Katie said she normally does not watch this type of program. She also does not watch war movies or anything showing violence.

The woman being interviewed was a survivor of the Hiroshima bombing and was relating her memories of the experience. She had been a child at the time and was in school on that fateful day. She said she remembered a great blinding light. She didn't know where it was coming from, and the people were running and screaming and things were crashing down.

The program used no footage of the bomb exploding or the aftermath, even though this practice is quite common in documentaries of this sort. There was only the woman talking. That was why Katie could never understand her radical reaction.

She said something just "clicked" inside her head and suddenly she could *see* what was happening. Horrified, she turned the TV off, but she couldn't turn off the pictures and scenes that flooded into her mind.

"I knew I was an old man and was watching from his viewpoint. I was feeling his feelings and thinking his thoughts. As I watched the scenes in my mind of the horror after the explosion, I knew that he was thinking, 'This can't be happening.' That someone couldn't do something that horrible. But mostly I remember what happened in the days afterward. Watching the children and the old people suffering and dying. And thinking that the people who died instantly got off so much easier because they didn't have to see the suffering. I know he did not die immediately, but lingered for about nine days. What I saw in my mind was a great emotional shock, a horrible experience. I couldn't understand what was happening to me. I don't know where it came from, but it was so *real.* I was really upset about it. I cried for days and days afterwards and went into a bad depression because I just couldn't handle it."

"Why do you think it hit you like that? Did you have the feeling you were there or what?" I asked.

She spoke with great emotion even now as she recalled the incident. "It wasn't a feeling; I *knew* it. Yet I was not even alive then, so it didn't make sense. I don't know how you know things that happen or that are going to happen. It's really something from within. You just know it. It was really a strange experience, because I am *not* a man now. But that was what felt *right.* I can't explain it any better."

"How did you finally come out of the depression?"

Katie sighed, "I just couldn't handle it, so I had to kind of push it back on itself. I knew that I would have to learn how to cope with it, but I couldn't handle it then."

"Does it bother you now?"

"I think I'm learning to cope with it a lot better now. I'm learning to think of it as if it happened to somebody else. I can take it out and look at it and maybe analyze it a little bit better. It's still … extremely painful."

I thought it would be similar to remembering painful events from your childhood and trying to understand more about them. She agreed, it was trying to find out the whys and wherefores, but this memory was much fresher than those from her childhood. It was an actual reliving, going through it as though it was happening at that moment, with all the emotions vivid and raw. The impact of something like this can only be imagined if you have not experienced it. This experience had a profound effect on her. She did not understand it, but she could not question the reality of it. The shock of it was basically why she had originally wanted to experience hypnotic regression. She was looking for an answer to explain this strange event, although she had not told me that until now. She was curious, but she was also afraid.

Even if she somehow had avoided seeing movies showing violence or war experiences, she must have known about the atomic bomb event from history. She answered, "Yes, but history is not alive until you see someone who has experienced it and you relive their pain. Then it becomes real and you feel it a lot more. This is the way I feel about this old man."

One thing was certain, the incident had come forth with such force, it must have some meaning and purpose for her conscious life. Otherwise, it would have remained hidden and concealed by the protective subconscious. But this experience had been too real for Katie. She had no desire to investigate it further. If the memory triggered by the television show had caused such emotion, she was afraid of what the actual reliving of the event through regression would do. She did not know if she would *ever* be ready to face it under hypnosis. I believed nothing would ever equal the initial shock that she had experienced when the memory was awakened. I was sure it would not be as traumatic under hypnosis because it could be controlled.

Something bothered me about Katie's strange experience. I could not understand why these memories of the atomic bomb had not been triggered before this. In our nuclear world, we have been exposed to stories and pictures of the event without our seeking them out. They have been a natural part of our lives ever since that horrendous event in 1945. I could not understand how she could have gone for 22 years without being affected.

Then something totally unexpected happened that may explain

her violent reaction to the film.

It occurred when she told me about her curious birth into her present life. Katie said that she had been born dead during a home delivery. The doctor tried, but had been unable to do anything for her, so he had put her limp body aside to concentrate his attention on Katie's mother. It was only through the intervention of Katie's aunt that she is alive at all. Although the doctor told them there was no use in trying, her aunt worked with the lifeless body for several long minutes, until finally a feeble cry was heard. Katie has been told this story all her life. The family fully believes that if it had not been for the aunt's perseverance, Katie would not be alive today.

Since I was biding time, trying to think of a way to uncover the Japanese experience, I thought this would be an interesting avenue to explore. I wanted to take Katie through her birth to find out why she had been born dead. I was positive there would be no ill effects. From past experience with this phenomenon, I believed that she was not even in the baby's body at the time of birth. She had delayed entry for some reason. It would be interesting to find out why she had been reluctant to enter this life. What I found totally unnerved me.

After she had been put into a deep trance, I asked her to go backward in her present life. Because of the circumstances of her birth, instead of asking her to go to the time she was born, I asked her to go to the time she first entered the physical body known as Kathryn H. Maybe it was this wording that triggered the incident. The subconscious interprets everything very literally.

Instead of preparing to enter the body of a newborn baby, I found her standing at the foot of a bed getting ready to enter the body of an adult. She was preparing to exchange places with the spirit that had inhabited the body of Katie for 21 years. That entity had taken on too many problems to be worked out during this lifetime and when she found that she was not strong enough to handle them, she had asked to be relieved of the situation. Because the two entities had known each other previously and had very similar personalities, they agreed to swap places for the remainder of the physical body's life. She assured me that this was quite proper and was done all the time, without the conscious mind being aware of it. This method was preferred over the highly objectionable method of suicide. The body must continue to live, even though the spirit wants to renege on its contract.

I had difficulty accepting this. I thought I had conducted so many regressions that there was nothing left to surprise me. But anytime we think we have all the answers, something always seems to happen to shake us from our smug complacency. We will probably never know everything and the search for knowledge will probably never be over. But to think that, as conscious human beings, we have so little to say about what is actually going on in our lives was a disturbing thought to me. It is as though our consciousness is but a thin veneer, covering an extremely complicated interior.

This puzzling situation sounded very much like what is called a "walk-in," a term that originated in Ruth Montgomery's writings and has come into popular usage. It loosely means a spirit that "walks-into" a living body, instead of being born into that body as a baby. I had encountered this phenomenon only once before in regressive hypnosis. That experience occurred in the 1960s, long before the term "walk-in" had even been coined, and was reported in my books *Five Lives Remembered,* and *Conversations with a Spirit.*

What bothered me the most was not the idea of Katie being a walk-in, but that she was such a recent one. If this exchange of spirits had occurred when she was 21, that meant it had happened just about six months before I met her. The idea was staggering to me. She seemed no different from anyone else I came into daily contact with. If this was to be believed, then nothing is as it seems. Maybe everything is but a façade. Just what is reality anyway? Does this mean we can never really know another person? Does it mean we can never really know ourselves? This situation impressed upon me quite strongly for the first time the separation of the different parts of a human being and how little control we truly have over these other parts. This sent my mind reeling. I must get used to the idea that anything can happen in this type of work and the unexpected and unusual is the norm rather than the exception.

Maybe this session held the answer to the question that had been bothering me. Maybe this was the explanation of why Katie's traumatic memory had not awakened before. She saw the TV interview early in 1982, shortly after she apparently walked-into this body. She had absorbed Katie's memories, but also carried her own past incarnation memories. Because she had entered so recently, these memories were still fresh in her mind. They had not had enough time to become dulled through the trauma of birth and growing up. To this new entity, it was as if the bombing of Hiroshima had just occurred, instead of actually happening almost 40 years before. The memory came flooding into her mind with so much fresh emotion that Katie had been overwhelmed.

I hesitated telling her what she had said while in trance. I didn't know if she needed any more complications in her life right now. But I felt that if she was not meant to know, her subconscious would have repressed this information.

When Katie came face-to-face with the idea of being a walk-in, she was startled, to say the least. She said she could not believe that. She felt no different and knew she was still the same person. She did say that her parents had remarked that she seemed different, that she had changed in the last year or so. But that could have been merely part of the natural maturing process. Her conscious mind rebelled at the idea and she had the same difficulty that I had in absorbing something of this magnitude. Since the story of her unusual birth was a well-known fact and had been retold many times within her family, it was obvious this walk-in information was the last thing she expected to come out during the regression. I told her if she did not want to accept the idea, she did not have to. She could just treat it as an interesting curiosity. This was not difficult for her to do, because it was not real to her. As a somnambulist, she did not remember anything she said while in trance.

Could this unexpected phenomenon also explain Katie's remarkable regressive somnambulistic ability? By not going through the involved birthing and growing-up processes, and by coming into the body recently, did she have fewer built-in blocks? Could this be why we were allowed easier access to her subconscious mind? This brought up interesting questions, but few answers.

Yes, this might possibly be the explanation for the sudden emergence of these memories, but at this point the cause seemed secondary. After the initial shock of this unexpected development began to wear off, I told myself I would have to push it aside for the moment. I would have to concentrate on Katie's problem—the real reason she had wanted to experience regression—to discover whether or not she had really been involved in the atomic explosion at Hiroshima in another life. That was the question that had bothered her and lurked, unbidden, in the background. I had to find a way of gaining access to the answers in order to set her mind at ease and lay the past to rest. But how was this to be accomplished?

Of course, in the back of my mind, I knew that if I were doing this solely from the curiosity of a writer and a researcher, I could bring forth this memory (if it did indeed exist) any time I wanted to. All I had to do was give her the keyword suggestion and take her there. I had been building a relationship with her and it was possible her subconscious would cooperate. Yes, I would get my story, but I would lose something much more important: Katie's trust. If I violated that, she would probably pull out of the sessions and be afraid to work with me again. It would indeed be the equivalent of rape (of the mind), to ignore her deep feelings and obtain information against her will. I knew I would have to take it a step at a time and do nothing to force her into a traumatic situation until she was ready, if indeed she ever would be.

Of course I was curious, but this was one of many times when patience was more important and would pay off. I had no way of knowing at that time that we were being tested. If I had handled this selfishly, none of the rich material that came afterwards would have ever been brought forth. It is as though the Jesus material (which I reported in my book, *Jesus and the Essenes*) was a reward, a crowning jewel given for the patient and understanding way these many other entities were dealt with.

Chapter 5

The Memory
Emerges

ONE DAY, before we began a session, I suggested we step inside that time period of the 1940s to see if there was anything there. We knew she had died as Sharon in Colorado in the late 1870s and been reborn as Katie in this present life in 1960. That was a gap of almost a hundred years. There was a possibility we might find another life there. It would be interesting to see if it was the Japanese one. Up until now, I had never directed her to a specific date. I had let her subconscious call the shots so she would feel in control of the situation. I told her I would pick a year that would not even be close to the war years and see what we found. Since this sounded safe, she agreed.

After the keyword put her into the familiar deep trance state, I told her to go to a happy day in the year 1935. This would be a neutral year before World War II began. If she was not alive then, she would say so. She might have been in the spirit resting place or at one of the schools on the astral plane. (These states of being are explored in my book *Conversations with a Spirit*.) I would have no influence over where she was.

I counted her back and asked what she was doing. She suddenly became a man in his late fifties making pottery at a kiln in back of his house. He was at his small farm located about 20 miles south of Hiroshima in Nippon (the Japanese word for Japan).

I can't say I was surprised to find him there. The memory had been so powerful and emotional to Katie, I believed it had to have come from a past life. I was pleased to have this verified.

Brad Steiger, noted author and reincarnation expert, has suggested that no research be done while you are working with a subject because of the slight possibility of knowledge being transferred via ESP. Thus I did no research on this Japanese lifetime until months after we had finished. I supposed I would have to rely on my old standby: books. They had not failed me yet. Book research is rewarding but slow. It always helps if you can find someone familiar with the subject you are researching. There were foreign students at the nearby college, but I thought they would probably not know any more about wartime conditions in Japan than the young people of our own country. By a brilliant stroke of luck, I happened to meet a woman who had spent five years in Japan and who had made a study of their history and customs. I am greatly indebted to her for her assistance. I have injected her findings, as well as my research, in the appropriate places in the story. The Japanese man's name was difficult for me to transcribe phonetically because the sound was foreign to my ear. When she listened to the tapes, she said his name was Nogorigatu.

The reader will note at times what appears to be mistakes in grammar, mistakes that Katie would not normally make. These are caused by the idiom used by the Japanese man in mental translation.

I began to establish the identity. I asked if his farm was very far from the ocean. He answered, "On an island, where can you get away from the ocean?" The farm consisted of three fields located in a valley. The nearest town was a small fishing village down by the bay. He could not see the ocean because his farm was between mountains. He had two sons, one 33 and the other 29, who lived with their families nearby and helped him and his wife raise the rice that was their main subsistence. I asked if he raised the rice to sell. Katie's voice took on a strange accent. She spoke in a crisp manner, chopping her words.

K: No, it is for us. Sometimes we trade it for other food.
D: *What else do you eat besides rice?*
K: Fish from the stream. Bean sprouts. Sometimes bamboo shoots, water chestnuts and peppers. We grow these in our garden.
D: *Then you don't have to buy much.*
K: No, our needs are few.
D: *Do you have any animals or livestock?*

K: Some goats and chickens.

D: *When you raise the rice, do you need animals to work the ground?*

K: My son has two oxen he uses to pull the plow. He keeps them there, yes.

I wanted to find out about the procedure for growing rice. I lived for two years in the Philippine Islands and I have always wondered why the fields were covered with water. I was sure Katie had no more knowledge of these things than I did.

K: It keeps other things from growing. The rice will grow in the water, and the weeds will not.

That sounded logical.

D: *When you are ready to harvest the rice, what do you do?*

K: First we drain the fields. All of the family helps. We go out in the fields, harvest it and bring it in to dry.

D: *Is it hard to drain the fields?*

K: We have watergates.

I asked about his house.

K: It is quite large, with seven rooms. One of the larger ones in the area. It has a southern exposure, a gray roof with pagoda gables. We have the sleeping chambers, one for my wife and myself. And then we have the rooms where my sons ... that were my sons'. And then we have the room in which has the brazier. And then we have the one that is more of a porch, the doors, they slide so that it can be either open or closed. And we have the room off back which we use to store things in. I have my pots and different things there ... it's where we keep the rice and food.

I asked about the eating arrangements and furniture.

K: We have a low table that we all sit at, one on each side. And we have our cushions that we kneel on. Sometimes you sit cross-legged, sometimes you kneel. It is up to personal comfort. Sometimes the top part of the wok is brought over and sat on the table. Sometimes we just fill our dishes and then sit down. Depending on how formal or informal the occasion warrants.

D: *How do you heat the house when it gets cold?*
K: We have little … stoves, little charcoal heaters that we utilize.
D: *You put them in each room?*
K: Yes, the ones that we are occupying at that time. And we utilize that; it is usually enough.
D: *What about when you want to take a bath?*
K: We use a big tub and then we fill it with water that we heat.
D: *Are you considered rich or poor?*
K: We are content.

Research showed very few Japanese farms were larger than a few acres. There is so little irrigable land that every bit is cultivated and used. There were few farm animals during that time period; most labor was done by hand. So Nogorigatu apparently was more well-to-do than the average farmer. This is also evident from the description of his house. Most farmers built their houses with sod roofs; his had pagoda gables and seven rooms. An interesting fact is the southern exposure—the Japanese never build their entrances facing north because they believe this will invite "evil." The room with the brazier was the kitchen area where the brazier was permanently in the floor in a well-type construction. The smaller charcoal heaters were filled with coals from this larger brazier and then taken to the other rooms. The room that was like a porch with sliding doors was used for ventilation, to allow air to enter in the summer and to shut off the air in the winter. I have been told that the description of the house was totally accurate.

I asked about the type of clothing he was wearing. He said he had on a gi (phonetic), which was a shirt that was wrapped and tied with a belt and worn with shortened pants. He wore this type when he was working and a kimono when he dressed up. I found that this gi is the same type of costume worn in the u.s. by people learning and practicing karate. It is a common article of clothing in Japan and is worn by all the men in their everyday affairs. The kimono is more formal.

Since he was working on making pottery, I wanted to know more about that. These are all subjects that I had no knowledge of, so I concentrated on asking questions about things that were alien to me. In later sessions, many times I was to find him working on what he affectionately called "my pots." He was making a vase the first time I found him.

K:　It is circular. It has red ash, was fired with colors dripped down.
D:　*Why do you make the pots?*
K:　I sell them in the city. I have sold it as far as Tokyo, but mostly I sell it in Hiroshima. At the open market, usually. We have a stand that is ours.

He said Hiroshima was about 20 miles away, and they usually went only once a month, having the oxen pull the cart.

D:　*Do you stay in the city until you sell everything?*
K:　Sometimes. Sometimes we just stay for one day, sometimes we stay for two. It depends on how everything is going. I usually stay with my cousin. He lives there. Usually it is just I, and my sons stay to work on the farm.
D:　*Since you don't sell your rice, is your pottery the only thing you have to raise money?*
K:　Yes.
D:　*Are you good at making pots?*
K:　In my way. Many say so. It is my life.
D:　*Do people pay very much for your pottery?*
K:　It is enough to be comfortable.
D:　*I mean, is it expensive?*
K:　Beauty usually is.

I was trying to get an amount in Japanese money, which I was sure Katie would not consciously know anything about. I have found that this evasive way of speaking was very typical of the Japanese.

D:　*Do you make anything besides pots?*
K:　Sometimes I make pottery bowls. Like Kuu-wan-yen, sometimes I make those.

I thought at first he had said Kwannon, the name of the goddess of mercy. This was why I asked the next question.

D: *Do you ever make little Buddhas, or figures of the gods or goddesses?*

K: No. I see no reason to. There are others who ... that is their work. Why should I interfere with it when I have my desire to create these images. I only create what I believe is beautiful.

If the word had actually been Kwannon, then this would have been a direct contradiction. When I showed this transcript to the woman who helped with the Japanese information, she said the word was not Kwannon, but Kuu-wan-yen. This is a bowl that is placed on the family altar and money or food is put in it as an offering to the gods. She said it would have been very possible that he could have made these.

D: *What kind of figures do you make?*

K: Figures out of clay. Animals, sometimes flowers, sometimes things in nature, like mountains.

D: *Do these sell well?*

K: Usually. It depends on the mood of the crowd. What people are looking for. The figures are really meant for me. I make them for their beauty. They please me.

D: *Does it take long to make the pottery?*

K: It is not fast work. One must get everything just right. If one hurries it, you end up with just broken shards.

D: *Where do you get the colors you use in the pottery?*

K: Sometimes from the herbs, sometimes from the mud in the creek. Sometimes I buy them, but more than likely I find them. Use things in nature. After they've dried, then they are powdered. You powder them and sometimes mix with water, sometimes other things.

This was a new idea for me. I didn't know you could make colors from herbs.

D: *What do you call the different herbs that make the best colors?*

K: I just find them. There are different ones. I don't know what they are called.

D: *That takes a lot of knowledge to know which ones. What colors do they make?*

K: Sometimes green, sometimes bright red. Some are blues.

D: *What colors do you have to buy?*

K: Mostly the dark blues.

D: *Do you put designs on the pots?*

K: I pour the dye or grays into the pot and twirl it. Where it falls. That is the design.

D: *Then you don't draw designs. … This country, does it have a king or a …*

K: (Interrupting) It has an Emperor. (I asked his name, and there was a long pause.) The Emperor is the Sun. I don't remember his name. Who pays attention to politics; they change. Politics makes you worry. I live my life in peace.

The Japanese people believe that the Emperor is the Sun God incarnate.

D: *Do you have much news about what is happening in the world?*

K: No, the world leaves me alone and I leave the world alone.

So Katie's triggered memories were accurate. We had established that she had indeed been alive during this time period. She was a Japanese man and had lived close to one of the infamous sites of the wartime bombings. But was 20 miles close enough to get the effects of the A-bomb? At this time I knew very little about the atomic explosion.

After this session I asked what her reactions were now that we had found there really was a man living there in Japan. Was she surprised, or had she more or less expected it?

"My reactions? Mixed, to say the least," she laughed. "In the back of my mind I could say, 'Well, maybe.' But I didn't really want to admit it could be possible. Even with the emotion the TV show triggered, I could always say, 'Wow, you certainly have a wild imagination.' It was really a strange feeling having it more or less confirmed."

I said, "Maybe you died of radiation exposure while living at the farm. But could that happen 20 miles away?"

She replied emphatically, "No, I was *in* Hiroshima at that time. I know it!"

I wanted to learn more about this man. If he had indeed died in this manner, how did he come to be in Hiroshima?

So, deep within Katie, a memory with no rational explanation had been bothering her for about six months before we had met and begun our sessions. She knew she was an old man and that he was in Hiroshima when the bomb exploded. She knew the man did not die immediately, but had lingered for nine days. Her most vivid recollection, and the one that haunted her the most, was hearing others dying. This brought out feelings of frustration and anger. She could not imagine how someone could do such a thing, to bring so much pain and suffering to other people. The memory of the others' cries was what had triggered her own crying and the depression that lasted for several days. From time to time the incident had come forward enough to cause her to seek an answer, and this was the basic reason for trying past-life regression. Would we find the answers? Her conscious mind associated so much trauma with the incident that she had no desire to repeat it. But would her curiosity win out? Neither of us had any idea what to expect, but it was certain we wanted to continue.

When the woman who helped me studied the transcript, she said there was an extreme amount of accuracy. Though some of Katie's descriptions are simplified, she could find no fault in them. They were full of little details that could not be obtained by research, but only by someone who had actually lived in Japan. As Katie and I worked together on this past life, we were to uncover a very real person who possessed all the complex emotions that mold us into human beings. This was no cardboard imaginary character. He was to become so real to me that he later began to haunt me, to prod me to tell his story. I came to know Nogorigatu very well. I liked him and he became my friend. I often wonder what he thought of me. Was I just a still, small voice in his head asking questions? I feel I shared a very vital experience with him, and if my presence there helped him in any way to accept and go through the ordeal, then I am grateful for the opportunity.

Chapter 6

Childhood

EVEN IF WE WOULD NEVER BE ABLE to explore Norgorigatu's death, this was a unique opportunity to find information about Japan. Since I had never had anyone regress to a Japanese lifetime before, my insatiable curiosity took over. I always want to find out everything I possibly can about any time period or culture I happen across. I ask many questions and try to cover every facet I can think of. This makes lots of work later when I begin my research, but it is worth it in the long run. My questioning also acts as a test because it raises the chance for error when you are asking about something totally unfamiliar.

One safe way to explore this life without experiencing trauma would be to go back to Nogorigatu's childhood. This way Katie could become comfortable with the personality. The story could not be rushed; I knew it would be obtained more easily through patience.

D: *Did you ever go to school?*

K: Yes. I started when I was seven and my last year was ... I believe I was 12, 13. Three or four or five years. I don't remember. It's been a long time. Most of our learning is "hands on." You must learn a trade as an apprentice. Usually that is learned from your father, or maybe a grandfather or sometimes even a cousin, if they have no sons. Perhaps you may decide that you want to foster one of the sons out, if that is what they wish, so they may learn a different trade.

D: *Is that what an apprentice means, learning from someone else?*

K: Yes, someone who is a master at that craft who is teaching you, yes.

D: *It is good to pass on your knowledge.*

K: This way something of yourself continues on, even after you have gone.

D: *Do you spend many years learning?*

K: Depends on how slow you are and it also depends on what you are studying. Different things require much more knowledge than some others. Like to become a farmer would not be as disciplining as an artist or a painter.

D: *Then your craft, making pottery, takes longer to learn, is that right?*

K: Yes, it took me several years. You learn the beginnings, and you learn how to form things. You learn of glazes and how to make them. How to fire things and how to know if it is fired right or if it must stay in longer. Because once it is out and cooled, that is it. You cannot put it back in.

I wanted to see what a Japanese school of that era would be like, so I counted him back to when he was around 11 years old and attending school. I asked him to tell me what he saw.

K: There are low tables, in which we all sit at one, and we have an ink pot and brushes. (The voice was noticeably younger.)

D: *You are all at one table?*

K: No, each has a small table in which we sit. Sometimes there are as many as 16 of us, sometimes there are as few as eight or nine, depending on who is needed at home. We are each learning at our own level of learning. We aren't learning the same things. Some of us are learning writing and reading, some math. We have a few books. A lot of the learning is done on … scrolls, I guess. Papers that have been rolled up and then bound.

D: *Do you read from these or use them to practice your writing?*

K: Both. We have leaflets of paper on which we practice our writing, using the brushes.

D: *Is it hard to learn to write?*

K: (Laughing) None of it is easy. You spread a line here or there. My brush strokes are not very good, and I make blotches and they mean something else. A dot in the wrong place. (Laughs again.) Some of us spend all of our years in school just learning to write. Otherwise it's just scribbles.

D: *I've heard there are many characters.*

K: There are ... somewhere around three or four thousand, I think. I don't know.

There are actually about 20,000 characters, but to a child even 4,000 would seem an enormous amount.

D: *Do you have more than one teacher?*

K: We have one. It is a man.

D: *Do you like him?*

K: He is very strict. It is very hard to like or dislike. It is hard to have an opinion of him. He is ... (sigh) ah, I don't know, he is just very fair.

D: *He's strictly a teacher, in other words. You wouldn't think of him in any other way?*

K: Yes, you would not meet him on the level as a friend, so therefore it is hard to judge.

D: *Is the school very far from where you live?*

K: No, it is in the village. Maybe a mile, maybe less, maybe more. It's right around there.

D: *Does anyone else in your family go to school with you?*

K: Yes, my brother. It is all the children who are of the age to learn to go to school, who are not needed at home. It is usually between the ages of six or seven, and if they are lucky, they get to go to maybe 14. But usually, it is only maybe 12 or 13, depending on how long you can be spared. As you get older, sometimes you are needed more often at home. And they figure that you have learned much from school and can learn more, like your father's trade or whatever. Everyone learns.

D: *Do girls go to school, too?*

K: Not in my school.

I didn't think so, but I thought I should ask anyway.

D: *Would there be a reason why a girl wouldn't go?*

K: I don't know. ... I just know that we don't have any girls.

D: *If a girl wanted to go, would she be allowed to?*

K: Probably not. Mostly, they, I think are taught by their mothers. I don't have any sisters so I don't know. I have three brothers.

D: *Do you like school?*

K: Umm ... it is interesting. We get to learn lots of new things and be with other people, but it is not my favorite occupation. It takes up too much of my day.

D: *How long do you go during the day?*

K: Umm, maybe five, six or seven hours. I don't know, not for sure. It varies sometimes from day to day too. As to how much needs to get done with what we are doing. I would rather go up in the hills and sketch things, and watch the animals. It is fun.

The woman who helped me with the research said Nogorigatu's family was obviously well-to-do. The lower class children of that time period (late 1800s) would not be allowed to rise above their status and would not attend school, unless it were one taught by the monks. Since each child in this school had his own table, this indicated it was a private school and his family paid tuition. Thus they had more than average income. Students did use brush and ink to write with and the books were mostly on scrolls. The leaflets were probably similar to scrap paper. The children did not have a set number of hours to attend during the day such as we are familiar with in our country. They stayed until the lesson was finished, no matter how long it took. Girls were not allowed to attend in those early days.

D: *Are you an apprentice yet?*

K: I'm learning a little with my father. Though he says, with my clumsy hands he wonders if I learn anything. (I laughed.) But, I'm learning the shapes and how to use the wheel. And different types of clays. Making different types of pots for different things, and it is very interesting.

D: *Do you think you will like the trade of pottery?*

K: Umm, probably. I like doing things with my hands.

D: *You said you also learn math?*

K: Some. We may have to do things like the books, because some of us will, you know, have budgets to work with. So they teach us how to balance things and add and subtract. Sometimes we use paper; sometimes we use the abacus. Different times; it depends on what you want to do.

D: *What else are they teaching you at school?*

K: What do you want to know? We're learning about Nippon and the history we have had. And they're teaching about ... the myths, I think you call them, of our beginnings. Just different histories and things. (This sounded interesting and I asked him to explain.) Well, they are legends about the way that Japan was formed, and how they are pearls that were cast into the sea and from them the islands sprung. There were a ... um, a god and a goddess and they liked this area so much that they decided they wanted to create a paradise, and this is what they formed. That is one of the different legends.

D: *Are there other ones?*

K: (Laughs) There are *many* legends. There are as many legends as there are probably monks in Japan. It's fun, yes. (I encouraged him to tell me more since I had not heard these stories.) They have all kind of different things about ... how that ... um, I can't remember the year ... Anyway, Japan was threatened with a hurricane and the Empress prayed to Kwannon (the goddess of mercy) and she saved Japan from being destroyed. There are many stories.

D: *Is this part of the history you have to learn?*

K: History, and just tales and legends, yes.

On another occasion when Nogorigatu emerged as a child, he was hiding in the woods watching the foxes play. He said there were times when his father would give him and his brothers a day to do whatever they wanted and he loved to go to the woods. This closeness to nature was to continue throughout his life.

Chapter 7

The Japanese
Wedding

BECAUSE NEITHER OF US KNEW anything about Japanese customs, I thought this would be an interesting avenue to explore. If she could accurately describe a culture we were so unfamiliar with, we could provide proof, not only that the life she was describing existed, but that reincarnation was the most possible explanation. This would also be a safe way to gain information without going near the questionable wartime period. I thought Nogorigatu's wedding day would be most appropriate, since weddings in any culture are full of local customs. I never told Katie in advance what I would ask about. Sometimes I didn't even know myself, because I never knew what kind of a situation we would encounter.

D: *Have you been married long?*
K: Since I was 14. We grow old together.
D: *Did you know your wife very long before you were married?*
K: We had never met. My parents saw her and thought she would make a good wife.
D: *(This seemed odd to me.) What did you think about that?*
K: It was acceptable.
D: *Were you married in a church?*
K: No, it was an outdoor ceremony and the priests came and they wore the red.

I counted Katie back to the day of the wedding and asked Nogorigatu to tell me what was happening. This would have been in the late 1800s.

K: I am dressing in the ceremonial kimono, and my father and my brothers help me. (A deep breath) I am scared! It is strange ... to know that I bring someone else into our house, who ... that I don't know this person. I know she is good because my parents picked her for me, but it is ... new.

The voice was definitely that of a younger person; it possessed a childish, almost innocent quality.

D: *Does she live near you?*
K: Yes, she lives about a village and a half ... in between the two villages.
D: *Have you ever seen her?*
K: Only once. We saw each other at the ceremony for the engagement. She looked proper, what can one say?
D: *(I laughed.) Were you allowed to speak with her?*
K: Yes, but I was too shy. She evidently felt the same way. She did not speak.
D: *What would have happened if you hadn't liked her?*
K: I would think my father would probably ... I don't know, he might have said we could call it off, but knowing father ... probably not.

Apparently, it would not even occur to the young people of that day to go against the wishes of their parents.

D: *How old are you now?*
K: Fourteen.
D: *And how old is she?*
K: She's about twelve and a half, I guess, maybe thirteen.
D: *Where will you live?*
K: With my parents.
D: *What kind of work do you do?*

K: I am apprentice to my father. He is a potter.

D: *Do you think it is hard work?*

K: What is work when you enjoy it? It is not work.

D: *Is that what you want to do with your life?*

K: It is a good life. He says that I show much promise, and that I have a good eye and a steady hand.

D: *Does your father make a good living at it?*

K: He makes a comfortable living. He has the land, and he has different—what do you say—rents from the people who are working them.

When I first encountered him as an adult, he said that he enjoyed making the little figures and selling them with his pots. He said they were more for his own enjoyment than profit. I wondered if he was making them as a child during his apprenticeship.

D: *Do you make those little figures?*

K: Zicooti? (Phonetic.) Sometimes. But my father doesn't know about them. I hide them. They are not what he would consider a useful spending of one's time. They're just playthings. They are mostly tiny little animals, like the frogs and sometimes the flowers.

D: *Well, I don't see anything wrong with that. I think if you enjoy it, you should do it.*

K: But they are not good for anything. They are not usable.

D: *Does everything have to be usable?*

K: In my father's eyes, yes.

He said he was dressing for the wedding, so I asked if there was a special type of clothes he had to wear.

K: It is a full kimono and obi. It is made out of silk. It is very fine. The silk of the kimono is in blues, with a black obi, with a little plum in the design. In the obi there are designs of some birds in flight.

The obi is the long, wide sash that is wound and tied around the waist on top of the kimono. One of the few things I do know about

Japanese customs is that the way the obi is tied has a meaning. One can tell by looking at the obi whether a person is married or single and many other things.

D: *Is the obi tied any certain way for a wedding?*
K: Yes. It has a double knot on it and it is very difficult. (He had difficulty finding the right words.) It has no edges showing. It is in back and is tied by my older brothers. It is not as if I can bend over backwards and tie it.
D: *(I laughed.) Do you wear anything on your head?*
K: For a while there is a black silk cap that I will wear. But that is only as I go. It is taken off while I am inside.
D: *What kind of shoes do you wear?*
K: They are sandals (has difficulty with that word) with silk straps that come between the toes. And platform ... what? ... geta on the bottom.

This is a type of shoe that is worn outside with built-up wooden platforms called geta to keep the wearer from getting his feet muddy. The flat slip-on shoes are worn mostly indoors.

D: *Are they special also?*
K: Just in the fact that they were made special with the silk, and the color that they are. They match the kimono.
D: *To me, it would seem difficult to walk on shoes like that.*
K: It is, but you learn with practice.
D: *Where are you going to have the wedding?*
K: We will go in a procession to the temple.
D: *Will the girl already be there?*
K: We will meet at the shrine, yes.

I moved him forward to the time of the ceremony and asked what was happening.

K: The priest is talking about our families, and our illustrious ancestors, and how that they are smiling down upon us. And he is putting a blessing over the both of us, so that we shall be joyful and fruitful and have many years together of happiness. And he will bind us together with the silk thread. (I asked him to explain.) It is a thread, one end is wrapped around my wrist, and then the other one is wrapped around hers. And it is tied so that they are both wrapped together and knotted, and then it is cut. This is to symbolize that our souls have been joined and that part of me is always with her and part of her is always with me. (I asked how the priest was dressed.) He has a very stiff silk robe, and it is ... not quite a kimono. It is ... I don't know, how do you explain it? ... something far greater. It is almost orange, between a yellow and orange type.

D: *Do they dress differently when they are performing a wedding?*

K: Yes, they have different robes for different ceremonies.

D: *What does the priest do after he cuts the silken thread?*

K: He sprinkles the incense and ... let's see ... sprinkles the water around, and blesses us. And then we have the procession off.

D: *It's not a very long ceremony?*

K: It can be, depending upon how much he wants to speak about our ancestors, and the match that we are making.

D: *Are you inside the temple?*

K: No, we're under the arch. It is a ... archway that has the names of the village ancestors, I guess you would call it, is carved on it, and it is blessed. It is part of the temple, but not inside the shrine itself. It is outside.

It surprised me that they were outside, but I found out they could be married anywhere they wished, as long as the priest was present. The archway was probably the torii, the square archway that stands at the entrance to a Shinto Temple. It could quite possibly have the names of the village ancestors carved on it. I asked how the bride was dressed.

K: She has a cherry blossom silk kimono, and her hair has the ceremonial knots with ... different things put on the head. The birds, and different things that are to do with the blessing of the couple for fertility ... and different symbols. In her ear she has symbols on her earrings that mean "good luck."

D: *What color is her obi?*

K: It is pink.

D: *Pink, with a cherry blossom kimono. Is her obi tied a certain way?*

K: Yes. Hers comes … it has the ends flowing down, and it is hard to describe. … It is in the back and it is a very intricate knot.

D: *Does she have her face covered?*

K: She has the white makeup on … pan, that is. And then just the outlining of the eyes and the lips.

Pan is the Japanese word for a flour made from rice powder. Was this what the makeup consisted of, or did it just look like flour to him? I had always been curious about this. I have seen movies where the dancers and actors wear the stark white makeup.

K: It is one of the traditions that has been brought down from the ancestors. A lady was supposed to be fair-skinned. Who knows?

D: *You mean it has something to do with an old story?*

K: Yes.

D: *Do you think the white makeup looks strange?*

K: I think it looks very nice.

I wondered if she had some kind of hat or something that covered her face.

K: No, not now.

Does this answer mean that she may have had one on before the ceremony and took if off, just as he said he had to remove his silk hat?

D: *Do you think she is happy about the occasion?*

K: Who can tell with girls?

D: *(I laughed.) Are you still scared?*

K: Not as badly. … (Then he tried to sound grown-up. I knew by his voice it was only a front.) Part of being a man. I think we will have a good marriage.

D: *Are there many people there?*

K: Yes, all my family and hers. Everyone to see us joined.

D: *Do your parents have to pay the priest to perform the ceremony? (Yes.) Is it expensive?*

K: I do not know, my father takes care of the money. It is whatever the family can afford.

D: *Well, after you have the procession out, is there any celebration or anything?*

K: Yes. When we return to the house we have the ceremony of the sake, in which she truly becomes a Japanese wife.

Sake is a Japanese wine made from rice, known to have a very high alcoholic content. I asked him to go forward to the celebration and tell me what was happening.

K: I take and pour into the cup a sip of sake, and I take a drink and hand it to her. Then she drinks it. Then another cup is poured, and the same thing happens. And on the third shared cup, she becomes my wife. And by that time, the sake ... Who cares?!

Katie smiled broadly. It was plain that by the third drink, they would really be feeling the effects of the sake.

D: *(I laughed.) Do all the people come back to the house?*

K: Yes, we are all happy and celebrating. There is music. They sing and there is some dancing. There are probably about four people playing. One does a harp. My cousin plays the koto. Someone on the drum, and there is a type of flute. ... What do you call it? (He tried to find the right words.) It is long and you blow in it. It kind of wraps around. It is very strange; it is called a ... it is not a bassoon, but it is very similar. (I asked if it was blown into like a flute.) No, it is a straight reed-type.

Research into musical instruments revealed that the instruments are correct. The koto is a guitar-like instrument, a lute with 13 strings. Drums are also used, as is the biwa, which is a harp-like instrument, a lyre with four strings. I thought the flute could be the shakuhachi but that is a straight flute. I could find nothing that fit the description Nogorigatu provided. But he did say it was strange-looking so it may have been an uncommon instrument.

D: *Do they have things to eat and drink?*

K: Yes. Lots and lots of sake and food—things that have been saved. There are honey cakes, and there are rice cakes, different things like that. Some sandwiches and rice dishes. Oh, weddings are nice times.

My research source said that when he said "things that have been saved," he meant they were made ahead of time and saved for the wedding. At first I thought the mention of sandwiches would be a mistake, since we have the impression that this is strictly an American custom. But the Japanese also eat sandwiches. Although they are made differently and are much smaller, they are still called sandwiches in translation.

D: *How long does the celebration go on?*

K: Usually way into the night. Then we are supposed to pretend to slip away and get caught and then are escorted into our room. Then everybody will leave.

D: *It is just the one-day celebration?*

K: Usually, yes. We are not rich enough to have it go on for a long time. Sometimes they have it go for a week, but it's not much work gets done.

D: *I think everyone would really be happy after a week.*

K: Yes, but then the morning after they stop drinking the sake, they would be very *un*happy.

D: *Have you drunk much sake before?*

K: Not much. Sometimes on ceremonies. That is not a child's drink.

D: *I bet by the time they take you to the room and they all leave, you are really feeling the sake, aren't you?*

K: (Katie was smiling.) Things begin to spin very rapidly.

D: *(I laughed.) Is this your bedroom or a special room?*

K: It is a new part of the house. It is just part of the grown-up's area that has been remade into our rooms. My room before was where those of us who had no wives lived.

D: *How many people are going to be living in your house now?*

K: We have my parents and my grandfather and my three brothers and their two wives and their children.

D: *Isn't that going to be a crowded house?*
K: Yes, but it is large enough; it will hold all.
D: *Well, this has been a happy day with many exciting things happening.*
K: Yes, I would say so.

When I awakened Katie after this wedding, a strange thing happened. She appeared confused, held her head and said she felt dizzy. She said she felt as if she had been "crashed on," in her words. I thought it might be only the normal confusion so often experienced upon awakening and becoming oriented again. It is very similar to waking up from a sound sleep. But I said jokingly, "Well, you *were* drinking a lot of sake."

She laughed and loudly remarked, "That's it! That's it! I feel like I have a hangover!"

So, in spite of my suggestions for well-being before awakening, she brought forward a hundred year old hangover. It was a case of the body remembering the life also, which occasionally happens. The physical sensations passed after about five minutes and we all had a good laugh. I then told her about Nogorigatu's experiences during the Japanese wedding.

My woman informant said that the wedding was extremely accurate. The obis were tied correctly and even the clothes were the right color. I would have thought the bride would wear white. I have seen pictures of modern Japanese brides in white kimonos, but apparently this is a custom that has been influenced by westernization. When Nogorigatu was married in the late 1800s, the cherry-blossom kimono would have been absolutely correct. The only thing I have been unable to check out was the tying of the silk thread around the wrists. I could find no mention of this anywhere. My informant said it sounded very Japanese and could very well have been a local custom, used only in the area in which he lived. It could also be an old custom that is no longer used. The drinking of the three sips of sake is still observed today. This is considered the official consummation of the wedding. When the traditional drinking is finished, the couple is considered married. Also, the pretending to run away and being brought back to their rooms is still done. It is amazing that the Japanese words which crept in were also accurate.

This whole episode is so accurate; it is impossible to believe the knowledge could have been obtained by any other method than actually reliving a valid memory. Katie has never been out of this country and had no interest in reading about things of this type. She could not have learned it from the limited amount of geography taught in our schools today. I have lived in the Philippines and have a few Japanese friends, but I knew nothing of these customs. That was my reason for asking these questions, to try to prove something neither of us had any knowledge of. It was quite exciting to have it all verified. I think the odds must be tremendous against all this happening by chance or by fantasy.

Chapter 8

Holidays and
Celebrations

I HAD DELIBERATELY NOT READ ANYTHING about Japan, wanting to get the information first-hand from Katie. Although my curiosity was killing me, I thought it best to wait until we had finished working with this life, so I would be unable to influence her in any way, even subconsciously through ESP. I could not pass up the opportunity to see what she could tell me about the Japanese people and their customs. My questions would concern things that were impossible for us to know without research. For instance, holidays and celebrations, since neither of us had any knowledge of these. I never told her in advance of a session what I would be asking about. I regressed her to the 1930s and began my questioning.

D: *Do you have any holidays or festivals that you celebrate where you live?*
K: They have the holidays of the gods, and then we have the birthdays of our ancestors that others celebrate, those of the Shinto. And there is, of course, the Emperor's birthday that everyone celebrates.
D: *Do you like the holidays?*
K: To me they are much the same. Why should any certain day be special? All days are special, and we should treat them as such, not setting aside just one day or two days a year that you celebrate.
D: *But on those days, do you do things that are different?*

K: Sometimes. Sometimes we dress and my sons and I and our families, we will go to the temple and celebrate with them. And they have the ceremonies, which are interesting.

D: *What is your favorite holiday?*

K: It is not a holiday that is my favorite. My favorite thing is the tea ceremony which is something that is rather special. (I asked him to describe it to me.) It is something that is among the family. And you go to the teahouse and the pot is full of the hot water, and you have the bowls. And you put the tea, all with great ceremony, into the bowl. And you use the brush and you stir it. And then the bowl is turned and the first tea is offered to the oldest person who is there. And with great ceremony, it is drunk. It goes through this again, and there are three times this is gone through, until everyone has gotten the tea. It is a ceremony of purification and just great joy.

D: *How often is this done?*

K: Oh, sometimes twice a month, sometimes more. It is when that someone has the time and everyone is together and willing to share this.

D: *A time together then. Is there any food or just the tea?*

K: Just the tea. Later we can eat, but the ceremony just has the tea.

D: *Where is the teahouse?*

K: It is a special building that is out in back of the house.

D: *Is it a very big building?*

K: No, it is quite small.

D: *Do you wear any special clothes while you are doing this?*

K: One of the ceremony kimonos.

Although simplified, the description of the tea ceremony has been proved completely accurate.

D: *This is your favorite. The other holidays, would you have to go to Hiroshima to observe them?*

K: Sometimes we go the temple that is in the village. And the other one is the temple in the mountains, which you can make a pilgrimage to. It is beautiful.

D: *What holiday would you go to the temple for?*

K: Mostly just the ones of the celebrations of the ancestors. For these we go to the ones in the mountains. We do not go often. Mostly they are religious holidays, and I still have very little use for priests. I believe there is an ultimate Being, but we must work our own path.

D: *Were you religious when you were younger?*

K: I was raised a Shinto.

D: *Why did you change your mind?*

K: It was just when the understanding came that ancestors long dead could not necessarily influence the actions of now. I later became a Buddhist, but I don't like the karmic systems of fate. (I asked him to explain.) Saying that man is ruled by his karma incurred before when he had … They say he has very little free will, and I believe that a man has free will to do what he wishes.

D: *Is this what this religion teaches? That man has no free will?*

K: That is what the priest wishes us to learn.

D: *Well, it seems you have a mind of your own and want to think for yourself.*

K: Don't we all? Why should you allow someone else to do something that could mean great challenges or change your lives entirely. Why should you let them influence your life? That should be your decision.

D: *There are many people who let others tell them what to think and what to do.*

K: Those are people with weak wills, and with little direction. … My parents are Shintos. In other words, they follow the religion of our ancestors. But they also follow the teachings of Buddha to a great extent. They both have their own solaces for the people who believe in them. They fill a need that most people have inside, and in this way they are good.

D: *Is it all right to believe in both religions?*

This idea is alien to us because in America we are used to people belonging to only one religion.

K: There is nothing really conflicting with either of those. They follow a lot of the same precepts.

D: *Are you Shinto, then?*
K: Maybe I am more Buddhist in the fact that I believe that we make
    a lot of our own destinies or problems through our own actions.
    I believe that there is a force in the universe, but I don't think that
    man has ever put a name to it. He has not gotten to the level of
    understanding so that he can become on a name basis with the
    power that is.

I had heard of the Buddhist religion, but not the Shinto. I have
since found that Buddhism involves reincarnation and karma, while
Shinto is concerned with honoring ancestors and living a life that
would make them proud. This of course is a simplified definition of
two complex religions. In Japan during the period we were looking
at, Shinto religion was the official state religion and during World
War II the religion took on patriotic overtones, much like the worship-
ping of their Emperor. Also, it was not uncommon for a Japanese to
believe in both religions as they spoke to different needs (patriotism
and personal morality).

D: *When you were growing up, were you taught religion?*
K: The priests, they have their shrines and we spend time as children
    talking to them and learning from them. Sometimes the teachers
    in the schools are priests. And then when we had religious obser-
    vances we would go, and we learned through our parents and the
    priests.
D: *Are there certain days that you would go to the temple?*

I was, of course, thinking of our observances of Sunday as a day
of worship.

K: There are certain ... like for the Buddhists, there are certain holi-
    days each year that one attends, different festivals. And for
    Shintoism there are also certain festivals and holidays. But also we
    celebrate our grandparent's-grandparent's-grandparent's birth-
    days and deaths. And thus, it makes it a personal observation of
    personal holidays.
D: *In the Christian religion Sunday is the day that they observe every*

week. Do you have a day like that when people go to the temples on a regular basis?

K: You said Sunday? ... um, it is not Sunday, it is ... Saturday. Sometimes we go then, but it is not always a regular basis. It is the day that no one is tilling the fields or doing a lot of work. The priest is always there and he is always celebrating the ... life, his observance of the religion, it goes on from day to day. It is like the Catholics, they have their ... mass from day to day, and it is like this.

D: *I see. Then Saturday would be considered your day of rest?*

K: Usually. Around my village and house, yes.

Here again, this has proved to be accurate. Saturday is the accepted day of rest in Japan. This is the day most shops are closed instead of Sunday. They do not go to the temples or shrines on a regular weekly basis such as we are used to in our form of church going.

D: *Then there is a similarity. But you are taught as a child in both religions?*

K: Yes. It is something that you grow up in, and most families that are Shinto have a family shrine that is in the house, and the observance of this is taught from the time we are young, yes.

D: *Then they wouldn't have to go to the large shrine?*

K: Not always, no. They have an altar in most Shinto houses at which we celebrate. (It sounded similar to the personal shrines in some Catholic homes. I asked for a description.) It has a bowl for the incense and it has a flat altar. And it has the scrolls of all of the ancestors, and whose families that have been married into, and different things like that. And it is all of our family's history.

Would this be any different from the people of our culture recording these things in the family Bible? I asked if some kind of ritual was performed.

K: You light the incense and you pray and you talk to them, and then you go over what they did in their lives and different things like that, yes.

D: *Is that done very often?*

K: Well … usually as often as someone remembers to do it. Maybe some families are more religious than mine. But in most it is this way.

D: *Then it is not uncommon for many of your people to have both faiths, the Buddhist and the Shinto?*

K: It is common since the coming of Buddhism, because it teaches a lot of things that add to being Shinto. And I have heard that there are even a few that follow the old religion and are Christians. It does not go as easily hand-in-hand.

This is called syncretism which means reconciling different systems of belief so that one is able to practice both religions.

D: *I think that is good. There is less conflict when you can have a little of all of them.*

I was surprised when I began to do research on the Japanese way of life, to find that many people are both Buddhist and Shinto in various mixtures. Usually this is influenced by the districts or areas of the country in which they live. If someone does not wish to believe or practice either religion, it is not frowned upon. Religion is not a requirement as it is in some Christian countries. The Japanese are very lenient about allowing people to believe or disbelieve anything they wish, although they have been harsher in times past on the Christian religion, seeing it not so much as a religion, but as a way of Westerners to exploit the country.

Chapter 9

The Marketplace in Hiroshima

DURING ONE SESSION, when I counted Katie to the year 1920, Nogorigatu was in the market in Hiroshima selling his pots. I asked him to give me a description of the marketplace.

K: It is open-air, and the people they have their booths that are set up. And they have whatever they are selling displayed on them, whether it is silks or foods, many things. And they are shouting. There is lots of noise and colors.

D: *It sounds like an exciting place.*

K: Yes, it is very enjoyable. The sun is shining. It is a very beautiful day. Many people to talk to and old friends to see. It is very good.

D: *What kind of pots are you selling?*

K: Many. They are made out of clay and they have the different shapes. I have very small ones and large ones and some pitchers, different types. Everything from everyday ware or very fancy ornamental ones with paintings on them. Flowers and sometimes animals—things like that.

This was the first time he had mentioned designs. When I first encountered him in the 1930s he was just decorating with dripped colors.

D: *How much do you charge for your pots?*

K: It varies from pot to pot. Mostly instead of selling them for money, people trade things. It depends on how much they can afford or what they want. There is no set price for just anyone. Bargaining is all part of the fun of having the market.

D: *Well, if someone were to give you money, how much would a pot sell for?*

K: Oh … the smaller ones, maybe a yen, maybe less. The larger ones … um, it depends on different things. What I feel at the time. Who knows?

D: *What is the most you ever received for a pot?*

K: Umm … maybe 40, 50 yen.

D: *That would be a good price?*

K: Not bad, yes, for a pot.

D: *If they were to trade something, what would it be?*

K: Sometimes people trade rice, maybe fish, different things like that. Sometimes cloth, sometimes pictures. Sometimes the artists come and they need things and they trade their pictures for things that I have. If I like them, I would keep them. If not, I would in turn trade them for something else or sell them.

I was curious to see if he could give me a description of Hiroshima, a city neither Katie or I knew anything about and one that has definitely been changed by the destruction of World War II.

D: *Is Hiroshima a big city?*

K: Fairly large. It has many factories and many people, and it's getting noisy and crowded. People have the fishing, and many shrines, many places that people go to worship. There are the parks. For a city it is not bad. It stays fairly clean. It is, I don't know … a noisy, cheerful place and the people are fairly cheerful.

D: *Would you like to live there?*

K: No, I do not like the confining. I like the open air and being able to go for walks in the hills and things like that.

D: *You said there are many shrines. What religion are these for?*

K: Different things. There is Shinto, and there is the Buddhist shrines, and they have many of the Christians. (That word was pronounced oddly, as though it was a strange word.) They have their churches and missions set up around the town. And there are even a few Hindu shrines.

D: *Then there are many in the city. Where is the marketplace located?*

K: It is well toward the southern part of town. It is not in the middle of town. It is, you know, towards the entrances as you would go into town. It is not far inside the city.

D: *When you speak of the entrance of the city, what do you mean?*

K: There are certain roads that lead into the city … four or five, I don't know. I have never been through the whole town. And you come in through those. It is like a main highway into the city.

D: *Does that one lead right to where the market is?*

K: It branches off a few times, but basically, yes.

D: *Do you go elsewhere in the city?*

K: Not usually. Usually I just go to the market and get the things I need and then I go home. Sometimes we stay for a couple of days. Usually I stay with my relatives. I have a cousin who lives in town, and he is willing to let me roll my mat in his house.

Since Hiroshima was so large, I have been told there had to be more than one marketplace. There would have been many located throughout the city. The people could not have been expected to come from the other side of town to get their goods. There would have been many smaller ones located throughout the city. The one Nogorigatu visited so frequently was probably a large commercial marketplace where merchants got products and took them to sell in the smaller markets.

D: *I think you told me once that you usually come to the market by oxen?*

K: Sometimes. Sometimes if I'm not coming to sell anything, I walk. Other times you can … if there is someone who has a truck or something that is coming into town, I can hitch a ride with them. When I come to sell, usually I take my cart and ox.

D: *Twenty miles seems like a long distance to walk.*

K: Yes, but it is something that is exciting to do and is different. Walking is good for you. You can look around and you can enjoy your surroundings. But it is not something I would want to do every day, or even very often.

D: *You mentioned fishing. Is Hiroshima near the water? (I really had no idea where Hiroshima was located.)*

K: It is a bay city, yes. It is actually on the delta. It has many branches of the river that runs through there. It is hard to get away from the water in Hiroshima. They have bridges. It is a city with many bridges.

D: *The branches of the river run through Hiroshima?*

K: Mostly toward the southern part of the city. And then they have the fishing base there where they have their docks.

D: *You said there are many factories, too?*

K: Yes, they bring things in, and they work with things like steel. And they make textiles and different things like that.

D: *It is really an industrialized city. (Yes.) But you'd rather stay in the country?*

K: Much. I prefer my peace and quiet.

At the time of his marriage, Nogorigatu lived with his family in another area. I wondered when and why he moved to the farm south of Hiroshima.

D: *Have you always lived out there in your house in the country?*

K: No, when I was younger we lived—maybe a half a day, two days away. It was my parent's land and my grandparents' before them.

D: *Then why did you move away?*

K: As I got older I wanted to see a little bit more of what was around. And I found this place and it sounded very beautiful and I decided to buy some land.

D: *Wouldn't you have inherited some of your parent's land eventually?*

K: Yes, and what I had I sold between my brothers and they divided it up and what I had from that I bought my land with.

D: *Did your parents object to this?*

K: No. They thought that it was very fair. I was not the oldest, so it did not matter if I stayed. Usually the oldest son always follows in the father's foot. And ... I don't know, he must do what tradition expects of him, I guess.

D: *The younger ones don't have to do that?*

K: Not as much so. There are more people who are moving away from the family homes and going into the cities and different things. And it is not as expected of them as it was, even 20 years ago.

D: *So you sold your land to your brothers and bought the place where you live now. Was it expensive?*

K: No, it was not that. It was only a few acres and there was no house on it. And there is really too much of a slope to be real good farm-land. But it had plenty of wood on it, and I was able to use the wood for my kiln. And it had a nice place where I could build on.

D: *What did you pay for it?*

K: I ... let me see; it was ... (a pause, as if thinking, then a laugh). It was many years ago. Umm ... somewhere around the price of maybe four or five oxen and a few goats. I don't remember. It was a barter.

D: *You didn't pay money for it?*

K: No. As in now there are still many things done in barter, and it was easier that way. Someone has something that you need or want and instead of worrying about money and how much it will cost, this is a much easier way of doing things.

D: *Oh, I thought if you sold your share of the land to your brothers for money, you would use that money to buy the land you have now.*

K: But see, I ... it was not actually money, but it was things of equiva-lent value, is what I got out of the deal. Because the brothers do not have the money to pay me off for my share, whatever is, and so they gave me something of theirs in trade for my part.

D: *I see, it is all done with trading. Did you build your house yourself?*

K: I hired some men to help me, but then I had my own design and we worked and we put it up, yes. It took about two months.

D: *Where did you live while it was being built?*

K: With some of the people in town. ... It was *good* to be able to work with something and show something that was progressing.

D: *You told me before you have two sons. Do they live with you?*

K: Yes. They help me with the work that I do. The pottery and the work on the land. We raise mostly what we eat and they help with that.

I asked about the names. He said his wife's name was Demadosan. His oldest son's name was Karatisa (phonetic), which he said meant "Joy of my joy." The youngest son was Nae (phonetic). I have always heard that Japanese names had a meaning, so I asked what his own name meant. This time he surprised me by giving me a different name than before.

K: Well, which one? My family name or *my* name?

I didn't know there were two. He paused as if to think of them. In hypnotic regressions, if often appears that the subject is trying to translate into English, as though their subconscious thinks this is a requirement.

D: *You said one is a family name?*
K: My parent's name, yes. Suragami. What you would consider the last name. Nogorigatu is my ... what you would call a given name.
D: *Do you know what those names mean?*
K: I used to. The names all have meanings. But in some cases, it has been so long since the name was given that sometimes it is no longer remembered.
D: *Do you go by your last name, as you call it?*
K: If someone is addressing me, they would call me Mister Suragami. But if someone is my friend, they would call me Nogorigatu.
D: I see. A stranger would use the last name and a friend would use the first name.

He had told me his given name from our first meeting. Apparently he considered me his friend.

Chapter 10

The War
Edges Closer

WE HAD ESTABLISHED that Katie's reawakened memories were correct. She had indeed lived a life as a man in Japan. It was still not clear how he came to be in Hiroshima at the time of the explosion. She was certain he had died there from the bomb instead of possible radiation fallout at his farm 20 miles to the south. He periodically traveled there to sell his wares in the marketplace, and I assumed this was what put "the victim at the scene of the crime," so to speak. He was probably just in the wrong place at the wrong time.

In establishing her presence in Japan, I had carefully avoided the war years, regressing Katie only to the "safe" times—Nogorigatu's childhood, marriage and the years through the 1930s. After many sessions I thought we were at last ready to step inside the war years, which began with the Japanese sneak attack on Pearl Harbor, December 7, 1941. I would still steer clear of the fatal year of 1945.

I counted her back to 1942. She said it was spring and they were in the field, watching the water wheel. During an earlier session she had referred to a water gate. I thought these were two names for the same thing, but I found they are two different things that are used to control the water.

D: *What do you use the water wheel for?*
K: It regulates the flow of water from the stream into the rice fields, and we are letting the water rise. We have the ditches that are dug,

and as we turn it, it lets more or less water in. When it is about a little over the ankle deep, if it is covering everything, that is enough water.

D: *Do you keep adding more water as it evaporates?*

K: Yes. It keeps the things that we don't want to grow out of it. Only rice will grow in a field with water.

D: *Is there water in the field when you are planting the rice?*

K: No, you drain it off. You let it dry for awhile, then you furrow your ground and you plant it. You let it grow for a little while, and then flood the field. It just makes it easier, you don't have to pull weeds or anything else.

D: *Do you have to go into the field while it's growing?*

K: Yes. To check and make sure there is nothing coming along and eating the plants. Animals come along, things like that. And to see how it's growing. Plus you must fertilize the plants. The water washes a lot of it away.

D: *What do you use for fertilizer?*

K: Usually animal dung.

D: *What do you do when you are ready to harvest the rice?*

K: Then you drain it off and then you harvest it and dry it and hull it and store it.

D: *Is it hard to hull?*

K: We use the forks and toss it up, and it blows away.

This is apparently the hull or chaff. I thought maybe there was some kind of machine that would do it.

D: *It sounds like hard work?*

K: Yes, but it is good.

I believe only someone who had actually grown and harvested rice would explain it in this manner. Nogorigatu was speaking from experience. He said his sons were with him helping him flood the fields.

K: My number one son, he's ... (Katie smiled broadly). He is called "my pain." (I laughed.) He is the one that is always arguing with me. He sees things in a modern way. He is always saying, let us do it *his* way because it is better. And that the old ways are wrong. He says I am an old man and do not know my own mind any more.

Apparently children have always rebelled against their parent's wishes and customs, no matter where they lived or in what time period. I asked him how he felt about his son's remarks.

K: I know that I know myself, and I know that it is the way of the young.

D: *What about your younger son? Does he argue with you too?*

K: No, he is quiet. He is a listener. He sits back and he listens and he watches.

D: *So you don't have many problems with him. How does your older son want to change things?*

K: He thinks that living off the land is old-fashioned, and he wants to move to Hiroshima. He thinks that the way of taking care of just ourselves is wrong. And that we should not ignore what goes on around us.

D: *How do you feel about that?*

K: If he must go, he will, but I will stay. I do not like the city. Everyone moves too fast. They are forgetting to care about others.

D: *Do you still go to Hiroshima to the market?*

K: Fewer and fewer times.

D: *Do you still make your pottery?*

K: Yes, and I sell it here and there. I make do.

D: *Do you need the money?*

K: No, I am well off. I am content.

D: *So you don't have to go to Hiroshima unless you want to.*

K: Less and less. There are too many other things. Everyone is involved in ... everything that is going on.

I was deliberately avoiding any mention of the war that had begun in the winter. I wanted him to tell me the story from his own point-of-view.

D: *What do you mean?*

K: (Sigh) They are always talking about how we were meant to be a great nation and that we must prove this. There is, uh … big change-overs which have been occurring lately in the government. There are two factions. One side thinks that we should become very, very strong. And the other side thinks, as I do, that we should just go on as we always have, keeping to ourselves and just living our lives. But the other side is growing strong. They have many people of influence. And, I don't know, sounds a little crazy to me. I was happy the way we were.

D: *Have you ever heard of the United States?*

K: Yes. It is a long way away. I know there are many here who do not like them, but they are far away.

D: *Do you think there will ever be any trouble between the two countries?*

K: Who knows? Hot tempers cool or they could rise up. Nothing is certain.

It was now obvious that Nogorigatu had no idea that his country was at war. With our modern mass news networks that constantly bombard us with the affairs of the world, this may be difficult to understand. But it could be possible, if he had been isolated on his farm through the winter and had not been to Hiroshima or the nearest village for a few months. In her normal waking state, Katie knew when the war began. So she was repressing knowledge that was readily available to her conscious mind. This was evidence of her complete identity with the other personality.

D: *Do you know what a radio is?*

K: Yes, there is one in town.

D: *Do you get any news of the world where you live?*

K: Some. Not much. Mostly I tend to ignore it. I live my life. Why should I worry about the world? It doesn't worry about me.

D: *(I had to laugh.) That's true. So, you are only concerned about your life on your farm. How does your wife feel about your number-one son wanting to move to the city and change things?*

K: Who knows. She says very little. She just listens and smiles a lot.

D: *So she doesn't express her opinions. Do your sons have families?*

K: The oldest one does. The youngest one, he has no children.

D: *What do their wives say about moving?*

K: It is the wife's place not to say anything. She just goes along with her husband. They are good girls.

D: *It seems as though women do not have any opinions. The man makes the decisions in the house?*

K: It is the nature of a male to be dominant.

D: *But you feel there is no reason to leave the farm?*

K: Not as far as I am concerned. My son says it is just because I am growing old and crazy. With age comes wisdom, not necessarily senility.

D: *Is your son very old?*

K: No. He's 39.

D: *But he thinks he knows more than you do. If he moved to Hiroshima what would he do to make a living?*

K: Probably work in one of the factories.

D: *Has he any training for that type of thing?*

K: Just as my apprentice, and what he has done in the field. There are a lot of them that are willing to train. This is what he is telling me. They need workers.

D: *What kind of a trade would they learn?*

K: Mostly working with putting things together. I'm not sure.

D: *Is that what they do in the factories?*

K: Who knows? A lot of dirty air comes out.

D: *(I laughed.) Have you ever been inside one of them?*

K: No. I've no wish to.

D: *Has your son? He seems to know about it.*

K: He says not, but sometimes I wonder.

D: *It would be a very different life, wouldn't it?*

K: Sounds like a crazy one to me. Once man gets away from the land, he creates all sorts of troubles for himself. One would think that he would long for the freedom of the fresh air, and being able to see the sky over one's head when he worked.

D: *Maybe they promised him a lot of money.*

K: And for this he would sell his soul?

It sounded like the same time-worn argument that is still going on between parents and children, when they try to rebel from the set pattern of their life.

D: *So this is what you argue about. But as you said, he will probably do what he wants anyway.*
K: Indubitably.
D: *What about your grandchildren?*

Katie always smiled at any mention of the grandchildren. It was obvious Nogorigatu had a deep affection for them.

K: They'd be like caged animals. Children are meant to grow up free, not in some small, box rooms. They need sunshine and fresh air.
D: *Do they go to school?*
K: Yes, in the village. They are teaching them all to read, to write.
D: *What kind of a school is it. A church school or ...*
K: (Interrupted) No, it is one of the state.

It was true that by this time the schools were controlled by the government. This allowed everyone to be taught, instead of just a privileged few.

The family was oblivious of their country being plunged into a war against a powerful enemy. They were involved with their own personal problems and he was jealously guarding his privacy. Of course, we also have no idea of how much information was being released to the Japanese people by their government.

During another session, when regressed to the springtime of 1943, Nogorigatu was sitting among the trees in the mountains behind his fields. This had often been a place he retreated to when he felt the need to be alone and to meditate upon his life. He had done this since he was a child. In such a setting, he loved to just be quiet and watch the animals and birds. I asked what was going on in his country at that time.

K: There is a lot of unrest and social problems. Having ... ah ... big groups ... where they take the men away, and train them to do with weapons or war with weapons.

D: *Why are they doing that?*

K: They say that our Japan is going to be one of the great countries of the world. That everyone will look up and respect us if we show them our strength. Who knows? I have no desire to fight. I think we should keep to ourselves. We have never needed anyone before but ourselves. Why should we bother with them now? We are doing fine. We should just take care of our own business and our own land and our own families.

D: *Are your sons there with you?*

K: Sometimes. My oldest son, he is ... sometimes he is here, sometimes he goes into the city and he works.

D: *What does he do there?*

K: Working in a factory of some sort. He won't tell us what he does there. Can't or won't, I don't know which. He doesn't talk about it at all. He likes the money it pays. He seems to think that that is important. I never ask about it. It is not my business. I have my land, my work.

D: *Did he ever say what he made while working there?*

K: I don't know. It was a part for ... I think a jeep or something. I'm not sure.

D: *Has he been working there long?*

K: Six, seven months, maybe a little longer. I don't know.

D: *What about his family?*

K: Right now they stay with me and my family, but he wants them to move into town with him. Soon he says he will spend most of his time there. (Sigh) I don't like it, but it's his life and I cannot live it for him. That is his choice. If I say that I want him to stay here, he would then just go out and do the complete opposite, just because I said this is what I wish. He is stubborn. A young bird must try his wings before he settles down.

D: *How many grandchildren do you have?*

K: Now I have three. They are very dear to me. I love them very much.

D: *What about your younger son?*

K: He has none, not yet, no. He cares for the land. It is good.

D: *The grandchildren are like the rewards.*

K: Oh, sometimes. Sometimes they are a trial. Growing times are very important. They must teach the children the values and to desire what is important in life.

D: *Yes, I agree. Do you still work at your pottery?*

K: Somewhat. I spend my time working in the fields or I'm trying to get things together, some things put away.

D: *For the winter?*

K: Just for whatever might come.

D: *Do you ever go into Hiroshima anymore to sell your pottery?*

I was still trying to understand how he came to be there at the time of the bombing.

K: Sometimes, but not often. Things are very, very tense. People are arguing about the problems that they are having. Some people are agreeing with what is going on, and others are disagreeing. And the ones that are in power are trying to make everyone listen to their point of view. And I just do not think it is worth the bother, too much arguing. I much prefer my peace. ... They say we must go forward. You cannot hold the clock back. But I do not think that strife is a way of going forward. I think it is a way of falling back. That is just my humble opinion. Everyone is entitled to their own viewpoint. ... The wars in Japan have made it a divided country, and we have not learned very much from them, from the past. We do not pay enough attention to what inner strife and stress with other people have caused.

D: *Has your country had wars before?*

K: Sometimes it seems like we are always at war. Either with ourselves or with others surrounding us ... people who want our land and our island. Sometimes I think there is no such thing as peace. It is all an illusion. There are always islands of peace. Man and his family, there is peace there, but the more powerful people have always wanted more power, and therefore there has always been wind and strife. If you look into our history, you will see it is a history of violence.

D: *Other countries have always wanted to take over?*

K: Not only other countries, but the people who have some small power want greater power. The desire for power begets more desire for power. The more you have the more you want.

D: *Has this trouble touched you yet?*

K: I have not let it. I close my eyes to things that I perhaps should not, and maybe it is wrong. But I live my existence as I wish to. I have no desire for strife so I tend to turn my head the other way. Which is not really good, because no matter how hard we wish it or will it to go, it is always there ready to creep up on us.

Without directly mentioning it, he seemed to infer that the country was at war. By not recognizing it, he was trying to be an isolationist. By pretending the trouble didn't exist, maybe it wouldn't bother him. As he had said once, "I leave the world alone, and the world leaves me alone." But he was about to find that it would *not* leave him alone. His world, the world as he knew it, was about to come crashing down on him.

Chapter 11

War Comes to
the Peaceful Man

DURING THE LAST SESSION, Nogorigatu seemed to be aware that
something different was happening in the country, but had been
untouched by it. If Katie's conscious mind had been influencing this
account, she would not have been so vague. She knew, as I did, some
of the history of those war years. I may have known more since I grew
up during that time, but it was obvious she was not tapping my subconscious either.

I suspected it was only a matter of time before Nogorigatu would
have to stop being a passive isolationist, so I moved him later into 1943
where I found him digging behind his house.

K: We are protecting our things. Many strangers and soldiers come
through and they take what they want. So we are hiding things.
D: *Your valuables?*
K: Yes, some of the jewelry, some of my pots and food.
D: *Why do they do this?*
K: Because they are in power and they are soldiers. When they come
through they take all of the supplies that they think that they need
and they do not leave us with very much.
D: *How do you feel about this?*
K: Very angry. They took our oxen and our goats and destroyed the
fields. It was a shortcut. They marched right through them, and
then they laughed.

D: *Wasn't there anything you could do about it?*

K: What could I do? I am an old man and they are many.

D: *Are your sons still there?*

K: (Sadly) No. They have gone … been taken away.

D: *Tell me what you mean.*

K: They've been made soldiers … for the glorious reign of Japan. (He almost spit out the last word.)

D: *When did this happen?*

K: A couple of months ago. They came and they stopped the trucks, and said that they had been … drafted. (He was obviously very upset.) And … they take them in the armies. And said that they were going to fight for the cause of our country. Some such nonsense. Who knows where they go. Somewhere out in the Pacific?

D: *How did your sons feel about this?*

K: They did not want to leave their homes and their families, but they were given no choice.

D: *Have you heard from them?*

K: No. They are not allowed to write home or do any visiting like this.

D: *When I talked to you before, you said your oldest son wanted to live in Hiroshima and work in the factory. Did he ever do that?*

K: For a while, but he learned that everything is not as easy as what they say it will be. He wanted to come back.

D: *Then you were right when you didn't want him to go.*

K: Yes … but it doesn't matter now. He came back to the farm for a while, and then he was taken away.

D: *Why are the soldiers there? What is going on in the country?*

K: They are keeping the so-called "dissidents" from revolting against what is going on. They want to show everyone that we have great strength. And they will make the people believe what they say by just telling them so.

D: *You mean the people in your part of Japan?*

K: Yes. Not everyone agrees with what is going on.

D: *What is going on?*

K: We are at war. (Katie's voice sounded as though Nogorigatu was in pain.)

D: *Oh? Who are you at war with?*

K: We are at war with Russia … and the United States. They have said that we are fighting … ah, they have formed what they call an … allegiance (hard to find the word) with Germany—we fight with them. I'm not sure. There is talk. I do not know, I do not listen. (Sigh) It is very depressing.

D: *Why did they go to war? Do you know what happened?*

K: (Sigh) Some general wanted to show his superiority over the Americans and he came up with a plan. And they destroyed an American base in the Pacific. And he says that this means that we will win the war because the Americans are just no good at war any more and that they are weak. And we will show them we are strong. It is a war of power. The people who talk to the Emperor, they have convinced him that Japan needs to be a great power, and they have the desire to have more power for more people. So they fight with others to gain this power that they have need of.

D: *What did you think when you heard about this?*

K: (Sigh) I think of all the death and destruction. There is no reason to kill others to gain the things that you wish. What can it win for you when you kill others to gain something for yourself? What enjoyment or good can there be out of this? No war is good. No one ever wins. (He again sounded very sad.) I cry for Nippon. She is fallen, she is losing her majesty.

D: *You know, I've always thought of Nippon as such a gentle, peaceful country. It seems strange that they could do such a thing.*

K: But the people, they are not peaceful. We have always had wars. No one is ever happy unless they are in power, and this is their way of showing themselves in power—this domination of those who are weaker than them or those who disagree with what they say.

D: *But Nippon is a small country in comparison with the world, do they really think they can do something like this?*

K: They are arrogant. They think that they shall fall greatly.

D: *Do you think the decision to do these things came from the general or from higher people?*

K: Well, they had a set of … council, and they decided that they did not like being played down upon by the rest of the world. They decided they would show the world that they were superior in warfare and skills and just general bravery, I guess.

D: *It seems an odd way to show it.*

K: They have determined not to lose face. Now that they have started on this path, they must continue on. They ... when there are problems *here,* they have to blame it on someone else. And this way they take it away from themselves, the blame, and put it somewhere else and say that it is their fault. It gives them a feeling of "We can unite the people in this great cause, and they will forget about their own problems." This is not good.

Apparently this strategy wasn't working very well, if they had to station their soldiers among the people to keep down rebellion. The war must have been unpopular with the common man.

D: *So they feel they can't back out. Did they have a big army to begin with?*

K: Not very large. Umm, I don't know how many. They are now amassing a—not an army—an air force, in which they recruit, (sneering) umph ... *recruit* people. (He apparently didn't think much of their methods.) In which they go on kamikaze missions and they are said to be blessed. I think they are a little crazy, maybe a little more than crazy.

D: *The way you said "recruit," you don't think the men wanted to go?*

K: No. A lot of it is ... they take young men who don't really have much purpose in life and convince them that this is the glorious purpose. And they are young enough and foolish enough to believe them. That is no choice.

D: *You said "kamikaze" missions. What is that?*

K: It is where they go and they never return—"divine wind." What they say is the god's will, that is why they call it "divine wind."

I had not heard this definition, but my research in the history of Japan disclosed that, in 1281, the Kublai Khan launched an immense flotilla against the island nation in retaliation for the beheading of their envoys. The ships were wrecked by a severe storm. The Japanese called the hurricane which saved them "kamikaze" (divine wind). During the war they called the suicide air squadrons by the same name. I knew the word but not the definition.

D: *You said they never return. Do you know what happens when they go on those missions?*

I wondered if he knew they were suicide missions in which the pilot deliberately crashed his plane into ships.

K: They die.
D: *You would think they wouldn't want to do that.*
K: Who knows what they have filled their minds with. What hopes of paradise. How can anyone promise something that they themselves have never seen?

This concepts is still being used in parts of the world today. Some militant Moslem factions are teaching their terrorists that to die for the "cause" will instantly position them in paradise upon their death.

D: *Are these things part of your country's religion?*
K: Somewhat. But they have warped it, so that it takes on their own method of being worked out.
D: *In other words, they have twisted the religious beliefs and made these young men believe these things?*
K: Yes, and their parents too. I have seen the mothers walking along with the belts for their sons, asking for prayers. Just old women; they feel they must get some comfort. They feel as if a part of them is going with their child, and they would have to feel better.

I found that there actually is something called a prayer belt or "thousand-stitch" belt. People would ask passersby on the street to sew stitches in a belt. These stitches represented prayers. When the thousandth stitch was completed, the belt, a white fabric that was tied around the head, was sent to a man at the fighting front. This was done in the belief that it would be protection against enemy bullets. These can be seen today in movies.

D: *So the soldiers came with the trucks and took both of your sons. Who is left there with you on the farm now?*
K: Just my wife and I.

D: *What happened to the grandchildren?*

K: They are with their mothers in the city. They felt that it was safer there than here. They are making them (the women) work in factories, and they can survive and have food that way.

D: *Wouldn't they have had food if they stayed with you?*

K: Yes, but this is not allowed. They need people to work in their factories and if they have taken all the men, there is just the women. And who cares about an old senile man like me?

D: *Then the women really didn't want to go to work in the factories?*

K: No. But if you don't work you don't eat. With the crops destroyed, couldn't eat much here. But we would have managed. We would have found a way.

D: *Did they come and take them?*

K: (Sarcastically) They showed them that this would be the acceptable way and then helped them move.

D: *Then they didn't give them any choice. Are they working in the same kind of factory that your oldest son worked in?*

K: I don't know. They won't tell me. They won't allow them to write to us. They say it is just for the government to know.

D: *Do you have any communication with them at all?*

K: Very infrequent. Sometimes they manage to get word that they are doing all right, but it is very hard.

Another example of the shutting off of communication. The average person must have known very little.

D: *Who takes care of the children?*

K: They have a center in which they take them. It is at the factory, and they watch them.

D: *I see. They take care of the children so the women can work in the factory. Are most of the men in the army?*

K: If they are young enough, yes.

D: *That doesn't leave many to care for the crops. How do they expect to feed the country and the army?*

K: Who knows? They will live off what they have stored and then they will starve.

D: *They aren't thinking very far in advance.*

K: They think they will win this war and it will be over with, and they will have no problems.

D: *You said the army, the soldiers that came through where you live are supposed to keep the people in line?*

K: Yes, and a show of strength. So that no one opens their mouth to say that this is wrong, or causes the people to think about it.

D: *So you think the people in general do not agree with what is happening?*

K: Why should anyone want being destroyed? The people do not make wars. It is the people in places of power who wish for more power. These are the ones who make wars. But what can we do? It is not something that anyone talks about. If they come out and say anything, this person disappears or is killed outright or ... you do not talk! Everyone agrees that things are not good, but we have no power—not the Emperor's ear—to be able to change things.

D: *Have you seen any examples of anything happening if someone spoke out?*

K: They will kill them.

D: *Their own people? That seems a bit drastic.*

K: When one is at war, one must have a unified front to present. If there is someone who is undermining this front, they feel they must be gotten rid of. (I asked for an example.) There was a man in the village. They say that he was caught stealing. I knew him. This man would never steal. He would starve first. I know that he was caught talking badly about those in power. And they took him out and they hung him.

D: *Did anyone say anything in his defense?*

K: No one dared. Because they all knew the truth, why he was being hung.

D: *Are these the orders that the soldiers have?*

K: Who knows? No one sees the orders but them, if there are any orders.

D: *Do you think they think of these things all by themselves?*

K: Perhaps. Who knows? Once you can get a show of strength and if you cow the people down enough, you won't have to worry about dealing with it again. That is why they have used this as an example.

D: *Make an example of someone and it frightens the other people. Do you have any way of defending yourself on the farm?*

K: My great-grandfather's sword, but that is all. No guns. They are all gone. That was on the list of things to be confiscated. They said no one that was a civilian was to be trusted with firearms.

D: *They took away your protection.*

K: But they say that *they* are the protection, so why should we worry. When it is them we must protect ourselves *from*.

D: *What else was on their list of things to take from the people?*

K: Whatever food stores that they could lay their hands on easily enough, that they could take with them, they took. Things like salted fish and rice, things that would keep.

D: *What do you think they will do with your goats and oxen?*

K: Probably kill them and use them for food. Now we have no way of plowing except by hand and I'm too old. But they don't care about this. They are not doing the work. That is part of the insanity that is going through. Every time that we start to grow things, something happens. Either the soldiers run through the fields or there is nothing to plant with, so it does no good.

D: *Do they have a camp nearby?*

K: Some miles away they have what they call their headquarters—a bunch of wooden huts that they threw together. It is above the town so they can watch it.

D: *Then I guess you see the soldiers from time to time.*

K: Hopefully I see them first, and then they won't see me. ... They haven't burnt anything yet. There are threats.

D: *Are you afraid they might do something like that?*

K: If things get bad enough, yes.

D: *Why would they do that?*

K: Who knows? They say something about if it is already done, then no one will want it or use it as a place to hide.

D: *That is odd logic. Why do they think you have to hide from them if they are the protectors?*

K: Who knows? Maybe they are thinking that if someone comes, I mean like as ... they are fighting in the north. Maybe that is what they think of.

D: *And the enemy, as they call it, won't be able to hide?*

K: I do not understand it but ... yes.

D: *Do you think that these other countries are the enemy?*

K: People should not be considered enemies; people are people. Maybe their beliefs and ideas do not come together or fit, but rather than fighting, they should sit down and talk about it. No one person in power can be good.

D: *Do you have bad feelings toward the United States?*

K: What are they to me? I have never been there. I do not even know what one—a person from there—is like. Is he any different from me? If you cut him, he bleeds? Do I not also? I have never seen an American, so how can I say that I can blame them for something that is happening to me, when they do not come over here and bother me. They have not done anything to me. How can someone be an enemy if I have never seen his face? He is not an enemy of my own making. This does not make sense. No, I have more grievances with the people who have destroyed my things, and taken my sons. Toward them I feel great anger.

D: *Is that why you are hiding some of your things, so you can have things to live on?*

K: Yes. We won't starve.

D: *Well, maybe your things will be safe. It is not good to have things all your life and have someone take them from you.*

K: No, it is very painful. Things that you care about.

D: *What about the other people? Do you think they will have food to eat?*

K: Who knows? Everyone is worried. The government says that they will take care of us, but I have my doubts. Anyone who lets soldiers destroy crops that are needed, can't know or realize much of what's going on.

He said it was now very late fall. They had harvested what they could and would be able to get through the winter.

D: *Maybe by spring you will be able to plant again.*

K: We hope. One can but hope.

D: *How does your wife feel about the situation?*

K: She does not say much, but I have seen her crying. I know she's worried and wonders what will happen to us, and to our sons. It's as if the whole world has gone insane, and we are just being pulled along with it.

D: *Do you think you'll be all right there or should you go to the city?*

K: I would rather die here than go into that city.

D: *Do you still make your pottery?*

K: Not often. We are worried more of day-to-day existence and keeping ourselves together.

D: *Well, you probably wouldn't have many places to sell it anyway. Do you need money?*

K: Not yet. We will manage. We always have.

I had assumed Nogorigatu was in Hiroshima selling his pots on the day the bomb was dropped. That was the most obvious conclusion, but he was no longer going there and he intended to stay away from the city. I would just have to go along with the story and find out what happened. I knew I was not influencing Katie in any way because every time I thought I had the answers they turned out to be wrong. I never knew what twists the story would take next.

D: *Will your daughters-in-law be paid for their jobs in the factory?*

K: Yes, and they will get food and a place to live. Not much more.

D: *Well, at least they'll be taken care of.*

K: So they say. I believe actions rather than words, and they have not earned my trust. So why should I trust them?

D: *This war that is going on, has it touched your country yet?*

K: They say that there are places in the north that are being destroyed, and there is fighting. So far there is none here. But we worry and wonder.

D: *At least you still have your wife. You have someone with you.*

K: For this I must be grateful. To know at least that I'm not alone.

So life was changing drastically for the peaceful man. The world was closing in on him. He was finding it increasingly difficult to ignore what was going on and to remain an isolationist. His world was falling apart around him. The Japanese government itself was aware of the unpopularity of the war, a fact that became obvious when they stationed the soldiers in the countryside to put down any hint of revolt among their own people. And the people were becoming disturbed by the stealing of food and the complete disruption of their private lives. Nogorigatu was presenting a story of Japan that I had never heard before and it surprised and disturbed me. I moved him forward to 1944 and asked what he saw. As he replied, Katie's voice dropped so low and soft I could barely hear him.

K: I see the grave of my wife.

This was a surprise. I asked for an explanation. The voice became filled with sorrow.

K: She was walking along the road in the village. And the jeeps came by and ran over her. They didn't see her and didn't care to. None of them stopped.
D: *Where were you at the time?*
K: I was at the house. ... She was begging. She was trying to get things for us to eat. Some rice. Anything.
D: *Don't you have any money anymore?*
K: Nothing that is accepted as money. You need *things,* and food is more important.
D: *Do you mean money is not valuable anymore?*
K: Only somewhat. Maybe in the cities. Out here, it is worthless.
D: *You said once that you had jewelry. Can you sell things like that?*
K: Yes, if I go into Hiroshima, maybe.
D: *But your wife was begging for food. She was going to bring it back to you? (A long pregnant pause.)*

Why did he let her go into the village by herself? Was he too proud to resort to begging? They had always been able to take care of themselves, relying on no one else. Was the fact that he let her go alone and she was killed as a result, becoming a burden of guilt for him?

D: *Weren't you able to grow anything?*
K: Some, but not enough. Every time it would grow, then someone would come and ruin the field or ... (very sadly) everything just seemed to go wrong.

It didn't make sense to me that a country would not want their farmers to grow food. It was the opposite here in the u.s. during the war.

D: *It would seem to me that they would want you to grow the food, then they could have some too.*

K: But *they* have food. They have things that they have stored that they have stolen from everyone. So why should they care if we starve?

You would think it would be better logic to let the farmer grow it and *then* take it. I wondered what the government intended to do when the supplies ran out, if no more was being grown.

D: *Then you have been eating what you had stored?*

K: Yes, and things that we find growing around here—berries, and roots and vegetables. Sometimes if I manage to catch a fox or maybe a rabbit, then we have meat.

D: *Is there any place to fish?*

K: Yes, but it is over-run with soldiers. It is not safe to go there.

D: *Well, what are you going to do now?*

K: (He seemed close to tears.) Who knows. Just sit and die. What does it matter?

D: *Are you going to stay there on the farm?*

K: Maybe, maybe not. Maybe I will go and live with my grand-children.

D: *Do you hear from your sons?*

K: Not in a long time.

D: *Do you know where they are?*

K: No, they're not allowed to say. Somewhere in the north. Who knows?

Katie's voice had become so sad and low it was difficult to under-stand. I thought she would start to cry. Nogorigatu seemed so incredibly unhappy. His grief was so fresh. It was apparent his wife had not been dead very long.

At one time, he had said he would never go to live in the city. He must have really been at the end of his rope, with no other choices open to him. Of course, at this point, nothing seemed to matter to him anyway.

D: *I thought you didn't like the city. How do you feel about having to go and live there?*

K: I don't want to. I feel badly about leaving this place. It's my life.

D: *Well, at least you will have food.*

K: (Angrily) Yes. No principles—but food. (A long sad pause.) We must all walk our own ways, our own path. If this is mine, so be it.

D: *It sounds like Japan is having a hard time. Has the war touched your country yet? (I was thinking of bombings.)*

K: Yes.

He spoke slowly and appeared to be groping and having difficulty finding the right words. It was as though he was so engrossed in his grief, he didn't want to talk about anything.

K: They are building protections ... shelters ... in which people would escape into in case of attack. They are being built around larger cities and the headquarters of the armies.

D: *How do they think they might be attacked?*

K: I don't know. Some say that it will come from the sea, some say that it will come from the air. People are afraid.

D: *Why doesn't the government stop this thing?*

K: It has gone too far. They cannot even if they have a desire to. They still believe in their own way that they can win. ... *No one wins.* I think it is all very senseless and very wrong. I just want my life of peace back.

D: *Yes, I can understand that.*

He was exhibiting such deep, deep sadness and sorrow, it was overwhelming. I felt so sorry for him, this man I had come to know so well, that I could not leave him there. I could not, in good conscience, end the session on such an unhappy note. Maybe it was more for my benefit that Katie's, because upon awakening she would have no conscious memory of the events she described. Whatever the reason, I decided to return Nogorigatu to a happier time before I awakened Katie. It seemed only fair, because to me he had become a real and sensitive human being, one capable of deep feelings and emotions. So I counted her back to 1930, to a peaceful time before the world had gone mad. Nogorigatu once again sounded younger and full of life.

K: They're having the procession through the village. It is the celebration of the blooming of the cherry trees. They have the priests at front, throwing the rice and calling blessings—hoping that this will be a good year for prosperity. And we have the young men and women of the village all dressed up in their most beautiful kimonos. They are wandering through the streets singing.

D: *Are you watching the procession or are you in it?*

K: No, I'm watching. I'm sitting on the hill away from it and I watch. I hear the flutes and the drums, and the cymbals and the bells. All the bells are ringing.

D: *Are there any decorations?*

K: Paper streamers and they have the kites that are flying from the houses. Things like that.

D: *Why do you celebrate the blooming of the cherry trees? Is that an important time?*

K: It is a time when one remembers that we live through the land, and the land must prosper.

How ironic that he should return to an occasion like that, when he had just experienced what happens when the land is not allowed to prosper, but rather stripped bare and lain fallow by thoughtless human beings.

D: *Is anyone with you?*

K: No, I watch it by myself. My family is in the procession and I watch them.

D: *Why didn't you want to be in it?*

K: I had no wish to. I just wanted to watch. They will get their enjoyment their way and I have mine in my own.

D: *It sounds like your family is happy.*

K: Very much so, I think.

D: *They are all dressed up in their nicest kimonos. And there's the music and the streamers. It is a very beautiful time and it will be a very happy memory.*

I was now able to bring Katie forward to the waking state with a clear conscience. I had reunited Nogorigatu with his family, even if only for a brief moment in time. I wanted him to remember the happy times rather than the bad ones. There are those who will say that it actually made no difference to him. He is long dead and I was merely reviving memories no matter what order I put them in. But I like to think that it *did* make a difference to this gentle man. If nothing else, it re-emphasized the building of trust between this entity and myself. Maybe somehow he could understand that I meant him only good, that I felt a great deal of compassion for him and his travails. Maybe this would help in our rapport as we inched closer to that fateful day when he would need every asset. Maybe this special feeling toward him was the only way the story could be drawn forth. I do not know. I only know I had developed a strange affection for this man and did not want him to suffer unduly at my hands. I would shield him from any unpleasantness, if it was in my power to do so.

Upon awakening from a session, Katie would feel fine. Because she was virtually asleep, she had no ill effects. *I* was the one who was troubled. I could not shut his suffering out as easily as she could. This man had begun to actually haunt me. His pain was my pain. I would hear again his words as I tried to sleep at night. He filled my waking thoughts, as well as my dreams. He became very real to me and it was as if his turmoil was happening now instead of 40 years ago. He seemed to be pleading with me to tell his story, to give his death meaning. Not to let him die in vain. I knew I had a job to do. Neither he nor I would have peace until his story was told. I felt his story was growing more important and I silently swore that I would grant his wish. It would be told.

Chapter 12

Wartime in

Hiroshima

I LEFT THAT LAST SESSION feeling very uneasy. Disturbing thoughts began to nag at my mind. As the story of this Japanese man unfolded, the picture he was giving me of his country and people during the war was one that I had never heard before. They were caught in a situation not of their own making. The horrors of war upon the people of a country was never more evident.

As I drove home after that last session, I was greatly troubled. There was something wrong that I couldn't quite put my finger on. Suddenly, like a flash of lightning illuminating everything on a dark night, I knew what it was. *My God!* I thought. We didn't need to drop that bomb! The country was falling apart internally. The people were starving to death. It was only a matter of time before the war would have been over anyway. There was no way a country in such turmoil could have held out much longer. It was an entirely new idea for me, a new way of thinking. It was a harsh revelation, but it had the indelible ring of truth.

Because I grew up during the war years, I had been exposed to all the propaganda in newspapers and movies. The enemy was the enemy—vile and monstrous—and there were no gray areas. In all the years since the ending of the war, I never once questioned whether the United States had done the right thing. It had just never entered my mind.

Now, for the first time in my life, I had to question the motives of my country. Why did we do it? Didn't we have spies inside Japan to tell us the true conditions there? Maybe not.

Maybe the experts didn't really know the country was on its knees. It helped me to think that. We are not perfect by any means; there have been black marks on our records before. But even the thought made me feel like a traitor and I felt deeply ashamed and depressed by what was flooding into my mind.

One thing I knew for sure, this version could not possibly be coming from Katie's conscious mind. If these ideas had not occurred to me, a person who was living during that wartime period, how could they have been thought up by a young girl who had not even been born then? As Katie and I were going to continue to work together, I had to put the disturbing thoughts to the background. The important thing was to get the Japanese man's story and relieve her of the burden of the horrifying memory that had been awakened. Surely later, when I began my research, I would find this was only one lonely old man's version and my country's reputation would emerge unscathed.

I was not even thinking these negative thoughts when we met the following week for our usual session. When Katie had been placed into the now familiar trance state, I again entered the war years and tried to edge closer to the time of the atomic explosion at Hiroshima. The poignant story of Nogorigatu continued to emerge. When his wife was killed by the soldiers, he had no will to live and did not know which way to turn. I counted Nogorigatu to the winter of 1944 and asked what he could see.

K: I can see the troops. They are moving. They have decided that they want the headquarters closer into town. So they have taken their troops and they are moving.

D: *Where are you?*

K: I have gone to my house to see my things.

D: *Are you still living in the house?*

K: Only sometimes. Sometimes I stay in the village, sometimes in Hiroshima.

D: *Can you see the troops from the house?*

K: Yes, they're on the road that goes to town. We try to keep away from the soldiers ... and hide.

Why did he say "we"? Did he mean the people in general were trying to keep out of the soldiers' sight?

D: *Who do you stay with when you are in Hiroshima?*
K: I stay with my daughters and my grandchildren. (He probably referred to them as his daughters because they were the only family he had left.) They work in the factories, and they go every day. The grandchildren are going to the government school, and being taken care of.

I had wondered from the first day we started on our adventure how he came to be in Hiroshima. Now I had the answer to my question. He had been forced to go to Hiroshima to live, something he swore he would never do. It could have been out of loneliness, desperation for food or a combination of the two. But we at last had the "victim at the scene of the crime," so to speak.

D: *Do you know what your daughters do in the factory?*
K: Some sort of work with the ... jeeps ... or something for parts of some sort. I'm not real sure. It is government business. ... All of the people who work in the factories, they live in the same area. This is several buildings that they have and that is where they live.
D: *Is there enough room for everyone when you are there?*
K: No, it is very close. They have two rooms that are theirs, and that is what they live in.

He was so used to the open air and freedom of his farm. This must have been a very difficult concession for him to make, to come and live in the crowded, noisy city.

K: There is many people who have come here ... away from the land, finding work and jobs. Things are very hard all over, so you take what you can get.
D: *Is there plenty of food in the city?*

K: They get a certain set amount of food for however many people, and you must make do. It is better for those who are working for the government than it is for the people who are still trying to go on with their lives as they had before the war.

D: *How do they get the food? Are they allowed to go to the market or what?*

I was thinking about the way food was rationed in the u.s. during the war. We were given ration books, but we used them to buy what we wanted or what was available from the grocery store.

K: They give the food to them in rations. They have a set amount and it is passed out.

D: *Is there enough to feed you too?*

K: We make it stretch. This is why I do not stay there always. I must learn to fend for myself. I am surviving.

D: *How do you travel back and forth?*

K: I must walk. It is a journey of about three days there and back.

D: *You must be a very healthy man to walk so far.*

K: One does what one must. A man can do anything if he sets his mind to it. Because no matter what, this is my home, even though I have had to leave it. This is where I belong. And sometimes I just need to come out here and spend time. Just to check and make sure that it is still standing, and that they haven't burned my house to the ground. ... It has been somewhat torn up. I do not know whether it is by people or just by the wind. Some of it I think, is people have been stealing part of the wood for their fires ... and they take things. There was not much left. A lot of the things I hid or buried, and they are still there. They will not do me much good now, but they are mine. There is no one who cares about ... things that I hold dear.

D: *There is nothing you could sell to buy food?*

K: No one wants to buy objects of art when it is war. They are more interested in quieting their empty stomachs, than looking at things with their eyes and appreciating the beauty. They have no value to anyone else but me.

D: *You told me one time that you buried some jewelry back there. Is that still there or did you use it?*

K: It is still there. I could never get rid of them. I think I would rather starve first. They have been passed down from generation to generation.

D: *(He seemed upset and I tried to reassure him.) Well, maybe some-day when everything is over, you will be able to come back and get it.*

K: We can but hope.

D: *(I changed the subject away from his sad memories.) Are there many troops along the road?*

K: Quite a few. They are all in their trucks and have their guns and they're moving.

D: *Do you know why they are moving their headquarters closer to town?*

K: No, I don't. One learns not to ask the military any questions if one wants to live. They have a feeling of importance if they know something that you do not.

D: *How do you feel about all these things that are going on?*

K: Confused. Wondering why they must happen. Someone must believe that they are doing what is right, but I cannot see this. I cannot see how anything good can come out of destroying people's lives. What is it worth? I mean, what price can we set on someone's life?

D: *What do the other people think?*

K: Most of them are as confused as I am. But mostly they are afraid to say much because they know that it is very dangerous to speak one's mind.

D: *Are the people in the city confused also?*

K: Some of them. They are mostly worried about their day-to-day existences, just keeping things together, to worry much about it. They at least have work and food.

D: *Are your daughters paid money?*

K: Yes, but in scrip. It is … you can only use it through the military and things like that. They are the ones who hold the key to the money.

I knew what scrip was. We used it while we were stationed in the Philippines. It is paper issued by the military in place of real money. Normally, it can only be used on government installations.

D: *You couldn't use this money to buy somewhere else?*

K: No, this is just through the military. They have their own stores, in which they have clothing and things like that. You must buy from them unless you go to the market and barter for things. You have something someone wants and you will have an open trade.

D: *That's interesting that they can control how you buy things as well as giving you the food rations.*

K: Well, you see, the more control they have over it, the more control they feel they have over the people. When you must buy solely through them, they can control you. You do not speak out against them because they would cut off your supplies.

D: *That's really taking away a lot of your freedom.*

K: What is freedom but a state of mind anyway?

D: *Well, before you were free to do what you wanted, more or less, weren't you?*

K: I was free to be ... left alone by the world, yes. The world encroaches, it seems to close around us. When you get down to a day-to-day level of struggle to survive, you do not have the ability to ignore the fact that problems exist. That is when you start thinking about things and what you've missed and wondering how you lost it in the first place. It is only at that point, when it becomes so severe, that people become aware that they ever lost anything.

D: *Well, from what you are saying, it doesn't sound like the government is worrying much about how the people are going to survive.*

K: To a large extent. They only worry about how *they* will survive. They think that if they win this situation, that they will have anything to choose from. And they will have plenty of supplies with which to feed the people and everyone will forget the hardships as before.

D: *What about the people who do not work in the factories? What do they do for food?*

K: Some of them use trade between others, and they make their own clothing and things like that and trade it for food, and different things. ... But there is lots of factory work for the government there, and there are a lot of military jobs. And most of the people are at least surviving.

D: *It sounds as though the ones who work in the factories have it better, to a certain extent.*

K: Umm, probably, because they know that their job is there. They don't have to worry about it. And of course, there's still the missionaries that they can go to, who get their supplies, and they help feed them.

D: *Where do the missionaries get their supplies?*

K: The Red Cross and others send them in, and they get supplies from them.

This surprised me, but I suppose the Red Cross has always been neutral, motivated strictly by humanitarian reasons. (The International Red Cross is a Swiss organization.) They were also allowed to send supplies into the prison camps during the war. I suppose it was possible that they sent supplies to Japan, but it was something I had never thought of and I do not believe it is common knowledge.

D: *Are these missionaries from the different religions?*

K: They have, you know, the Catholic priests and the Lutherans. They are able to help somewhat, yes.

D: *I wonder if the government really knows how bad things are?*

K: Or if they really care. Knowing and caring are two different things. They see this great idea of winning. They don't care what the cost is.

Katie began to show discomfort and I asked what was wrong. Nogorigatu said he was just tired, but sounded as though it was a tiredness of the soul, not the body. I took her out of that scene.

We had worked for weeks gathering the information about the life of this Japanese man. I only began to move inside the war years with her permission. I had been true to my promise and had not approached the fateful day of August 6, 1945, when the atomic bomb was dropped on Hiroshima. At the end of this session, I realized we had reached the end of the road. I told her there was only one place left to go—to explore Nogorigatu's death. She had already relived much trauma and sadness as the Japanese man related his experiences, and they had not affected her in the waking state at all. I knew she would never again experience the same upheaval that had occurred when the memory of the bombing first emerged. I felt that, under hypnosis, the telling of the story could be controlled and it would never again have the same impact on her conscious mind. I promised her, if she was agreeable to trying it, that we would do it one time only and never approach it again. Katie sat in deep thought, pondering the situation. She also realized we had gone as far as we could go in examining that lifetime. The only thing left to explore was the death. She couldn't give me an answer yet. She wanted to think about it during the week and would let me know when we met for our next usual session.

Chapter 13

The Atomic Bomb

THE NEXT WEEK, as I sat in my car waiting for Katie to get off work, many thoughts ran through my mind. The trust we had built was more important than obtaining an exciting story. Also, the Japanese man had become very real to me and I knew I could not betray him. This was as important to me as harming my relationship with Katie. I must consider *both* as real persons with feelings and emotions. We could always continue to explore other lives if she felt she was not yet ready to face this. I have never forced any of my subjects to do anything they were uncomfortable with.

When Katie approached the car, she was all smiles. She had made the decision to proceed and she felt as though a great weight had been lifted from her shoulders. She knew from somewhere deep inside that experiencing the death of Nogorigatu was very important to her well-being and must be faced. If she ran from it, she felt it would always be nagging at the back of her mind. But making the decision to confront it didn't mean that she was not afraid. She was still nervous about going through with it. It has been said that true bravery is doing something even though we are terrified. It takes no courage to do something easy. I was proud of her for making the decision, not for my sake, but hers. I felt it would be tremendously helpful in her spiritual growth.

At the house, as we got ready for the session, *I* began to be troubled. I had taken many, many people through their deaths during hypnotic regressions. Most of these had happened spontaneously with no warning. At other times, I had directed them to experience the death. I had always been able to control the amount of trauma encountered by the subject.

I knew what we would explore this day was a totally different circumstance. This was the first time I knew in advance how someone would die, and how it had already affected Katie in the waking state. Does anyone really know what it would be like to die from an atomic explosion? Would this death experience be different? How would she react? How would *I* react? The whole idea gave me the shivers. She instinctively picked up on my anxiety. "Hey, I don't know who's more nervous, you or me!"

I laughed, but I did not try to hide my feelings from her. I voiced my reservations, but she still felt she must go through with it. I knew from past experiences with other subjects that if it became too much for her to handle, she would wake up, just as you do from a nightmare. The subconscious protects the subject the entire time they are in the somnambulistic state and I would have no power to hold her there if she did not wish to reexperience it. When I used the keyword and watched her slip into the familiar trance state, I put the usual mental "white light of protection" around her. Only this time I also called in her spirit guides and the powers that surround us to help see her through this ordeal. (These are also called guardian angels by some people.) I did not want to leave anything to chance. I knew she would need all the help we could get.

During this session, I became so involved and was so concerned with monitoring Katie's physical reactions, I did not get the full emotional impact of the experience until I later played the tape recording. When I have played this tape for groups of interested people, many have cried and others could not sit through it. They rushed from the room. I hope I can convey this very real, heart-rending emotion through such a poor medium as the written word. I have agonized over the most effective way to express these feelings on paper. I feel there is something here that needs to be told. It is a story for our time and it cries out to our world. It beseeches, "Do not let this madness happen again!"

I took a deep breath and began.

D: *Let's go to the spring of 1945. It will be spring when the earth is waking up and things are beginning to grow again. What do you see?*

K: I can see the planes flying overhead. It seems like they are stalking us. They are watching what we do.

D: *Where are you?*

K: In Hiroshima.

D: *What kind of planes are they?*

K: Uh … I don't know. They are fairly large. There are … four or five of them and they fly overhead.

D: *Why are they flying over the city?*

K: I have no idea. They are not ours. But it's just as if they watch us. They do not drop bombs, they just watch. We have seen them before, but it is a recent thing they have started, coming and flying over. I wonder if they are looking for a good place to drop their bombs. I don't know.

D: *Have planes dropped bombs before?*

K: To the north and the surrounding areas, yes. They have dropped and caused much damage to fields and towns. We've never had any serious hits, at least not in the city. They keep things a secret. Maybe it is our turn next.

D: *Why are they dropping the bombs?*

K: This is the country we are at war with. This is the war that we have been fighting, only it has now come home.

D: *Do you think the government expected this to happen?*

K: Who knows. They probably thought that it would end before it ever got this far. Who am I to judge? I am not able to have their information. … It worries me, because I know if they are dropping things off and they are flying over our city, they could easily drop them on us. And I wonder.

D: *Are the people afraid when the planes fly over?*

K: Yes. They run and they have … shelters and things, places to go to make sure … They call it … bomb shelters, or something like that. I don't know. (He was confused about the word.)

D: *Have you ever been in one of them?*

K: Yes. Some of them are schools that are just well protected and maybe a little farther out from, away from the factories and things. Others are basements of taller buildings.

D: *This is where people go when the planes come?*

K: Sometimes, yes. Sometimes the people just go on about their business. They must live no matter what.

D: *Don't they have any set regulations about it?*

K: They have sirens, and as they go off, they have to scream the noise throughout the city that there is a possible attack pending. But so far no attack. You must clear the streets, but other than that there is no problem. I do not desire to go to the shelter. I would rather see what is coming at me than run like a frightened squirrel into a tree and hole up. If I die I would like to see what kills me.

D: *Do you still go back and forth to your home?*

K: No. It is too dangerous there with all the troops and possible bombings and … I don't go.

D: *Do you like living in the city with your daughters?*

K: I feel like a caged bird … who is confused and cannot fly.

D: *Are you able to go out for walks sometimes?*

K: Sometimes, but we get stopped in the street. They are suspicious of everyone. The soldiers ask questions. "Why are you here? What are you doing?" Everyone is getting very suspicious and edgy. Sometimes when I manage to get out, I go for walks, but there is nowhere to walk except in the town. I do not like it. I like living in my own house, having my fields and my animals around me. I miss the quiet and peacefulness.

D: *You said you only have two rooms. Is it hard for all of you to sleep?*

K: We spread the mats on the floors and we sleep on them, and there is enough room for that.

D: *Do you have a place to cook?*

K: We have a brazier, which is a charcoal one, that is in the one room.

D: *Well, at least you are not alone. That is something to be thankful for.*

K: Yes, this is true. But this is no life to bring up children in either.

D: *That is true. And this is … what month is this?*

K: This is April.

D: *April of 1945. Okay, let's go forward a few more months. It will be July of 1945. That is in the summer when it's hot.*

I didn't want to jump right in, believing it would be better to take our time and edge up on it. I counted forward to July, 1945, and asked what Nogorigatu saw.

K: I see my daughters as they come in from work. I'm helping them with the meal.

D: *How are things going?*

K: Things are extremely bad. There are many problems. They've had bombings around the city and everyone is worried and tense. There have been no direct hits here and we're always wondering when. Two of the outlying factories have been hit, no *serious* damage, some deaths. They manage to keep working.

D: *What does it sound like when the bombs drop? Can you hear them?*

K: There is a shrill whistle before the explosion. They say you never hear the one that hits, so I don't know.

D: *What about the factory your daughters work in? Has it had any damage yet?*

K: Not yet.

D: *The housing you are living in, is that close to the factory?*

K: Not real close, but close enough to be worried about.

D: *Do the planes come over very often?*

K: They come every morning, early in the morning. I watch them and I wonder ... when? Some people can ignore them (deep sigh); I cannot.

D: *Is there any of the army around there that could give protection?*

K: They fire at them. But they almost treat it as if a big game is going on. As if nothing serious. I ... I don't understand. (I asked him to explain.) Oh, it's as if they expect them and they take three shots at them with their guns and that's it. It's as if they don't care if they hit them, or maybe they're out of range. I don't know.

D: *Is it like this all over the country?*

K: I don't know. We don't get much news. The military is who gets the news and they do not tell us much.

D: *Do you still go to the bomb shelters?*

K: Sometimes. The people they ... it has become such a daily occurrence, they don't worry about it. (He laughed.) Some people say they set their clocks by the planes. (Becoming serious) I feel that this is some plan that they have. They are doing something. I do not think that they are foolish enough to be doing this every day for no reason. They are looking for something, or planning something. I don't know what.

D: *It does sound strange. I can see how it could get to the point where you don't really feel in danger.*

K: You ignore their existence, yes. Some people say that this is what they feel. They do not worry. (Sigh) *I* worry. They say I'm a foolish old man, but I worry.

D: *Do your daughters worry?*

K: They believe in what they are told. They say that the Americans don't wish to bomb us, or something ... I don't know. They say that they are not strong enough to fight us. They are saying that the war is almost over because we are no longer fighting with them. Who knows?

D: *It sounds like they tell you all kinds of things. ... Are the grandchildren afraid?*

K: No, they just watch the planes. They think that it is very interesting to get to watch the planes as they go over.

D: *How is the food holding out?*

K: We are still surviving on what they give us. I don't know where they are getting it from. It is mostly rice. It is less than what it used to be, but we are still making it. Sometimes if we are lucky we come upon some things in the open market. Bread, grains and ... that is about it. Sometimes we grow our own sprouts, if we are lucky enough to find the beans. We grow them in the rooms with a little water and sunlight, and we have them with the rice. Occasionally we have meat, but not very often. It is getting to be very rare.

D: *Does the meat come from the government or from the market?*

K: Sometimes a little bit of both. Sometimes we get some through our rations, but more likely we get it from someone who has slaughtered his oxen, or something like that.

D: *You told me before that you barter for things in the market. What do you use to trade with?*

K: Different things. Sometimes an extra blanket. Sometimes I go out and find fruit and nuts, things like that. So we trade them. Anything we can get our hands on.

D: *It sounds like money has no value anymore.*

K: No, not any real value. I have not seen any in a long time.

I found out that the black market was flourishing in Hiroshima (and probably all over Japan) during this time of the war.

D: *How do they allot the food to you?*

K: They give it to them at work, twice a week, usually.
D: It's a different existence than you were used to.
K: Yes, much harsher, more dealing with the realities.
D: … And you are helping prepare dinner?
K: I'm watching my three grandchildren. They are playing.
D: They are a blessing.
K: Yes, they take your mind off the problems sometimes, but then you worry about what will happen to them.

It was now or never, so I decided it was time to make the jump. I took a deep breath and plunged ahead.

D: We're going to leave that scene and move up a few more weeks. We are going to go forward to August 6, 1945, and you will tell me what you see. Remember, keep in your mind that you are covered with the white light of protection and your guide is here to help you. We will let nothing harm you in any way. Anything you see is only a memory and you can tell me about it. There is much to learn from it. But it will not bother you in any way mentally or physically. If you wish, you can always watch it as an observer.

As I counted Katie forward to that all-important day, her complexion suddenly changed. She turned white as a sheet and her body stiffened. She seemed to be in a state of confusion. When she tried to talk, only gasping sounds came out. She had great difficulty forming the words. The contrast between the former slow, curt, choppy speech of the Japanese and the present state of the entity was very marked. She seemed to be in a state of shock and when she did manage to speak, her voice trembled. Sometimes her body would shake. I had never before heard such heart-rendering emotion and pain in a voice. It came from somewhere deep inside her subconscious memories and had no connection with Katie at all.

It was obvious something drastic had happened. I was certain I knew what it was, but I had to proceed as if I didn't know anything, and let Nogorigatu tell his own story. Katie was taking deep breaths. I asked her what was happening.

She was finally able to speak, with difficulty. The phrases came out disjointed with pauses between them as Nogorigatu confusedly groped to find the words for an experience that words were useless to describe.

K: There was ... there was a great flash. And then the *winds* ... they were like fire. The people, they fell down, and they ... and they just lay there, and ... and ... (the voice was full of utter disbelief). *The screams!*
D: *Where are you watching from?*
K: I was in the market.
D: *Tell me what the flash was like.*
K: A blinding, white light. And ... and then a great ... boom. And ... and ... a *giant* cloud. It went straight up, and ... and ... it went out. And then the winds rolled. They were like fire! *People are dying everywhere! WHY?!*

It was a cry from the depths of his soul, and it sent shivers down my spine.

D: *What has happened, do you know?*

He couldn't get the sounds out. I had to reassure Katie, knowing that at any moment she might decide to terminate this and wake herself up. I spoke soothingly and lovingly to Nogorigatu, for I had truly come to have great compassion for this man. "You can talk about it. In fact, it would probably be good to talk about it because, you see, I understand."

K: I don't ... it's hard to hear anything but the *screams!* People are ... those who can run are running. People falling down. Some just stumbling around, holding their arms out. ... (The shock was rising close to panic.) Everything is gone! It's been destroyed! Buildings are as if they've never been! There's nothing left! *WHY?!*
D: *Are you by yourself or with your daughters?*
K: I am alone. (Bewildered) I don't know where *anyone* is. Everything is gone! The city is as if ... there is no *center* to the city! *IT'S*

GONE! The buildings have ... *disappeared!* There's nothing but rubble ... and the *screams!*

Even as I write these words I can hear again the complete horror in Katie's voice.

I had to keep myself from being caught up in this. Only by remaining objective would I be able to monitor her and think of questions to ask.

D: *Where is the market located?*

K: It was ... by one of the entrances into the town. It ... was away out ... from the center.

D: *You said the cloud rose straight up and then the winds came? Is that when the buildings began to disappear?*

K: Yes, and they ... the people, they fell. People just ... died.

D: *Did the buildings disappear when the cloud hit or the wind hit?*

K: Some of both. Some ... when the cloud hit, they ... disappeared in that moment. Some, the great wind, it knocked everything to the ground. All of the people ... (He paused, as if having difficulty completing sentences.)

D: *Did you fall down?*

K: Yes. ... It ... shrieked. I could not tell if it ... it was people screaming or if it was the noise. I don't ... I don't know. All I know is ... everyone is dying! (His voice trailed off in a painful whisper.)

There was a pause and I could tell by the movement of Katie's eyes under her eyelids that Nogorigatu was looking down. Unexpectedly, he blurted out, "My ... hands!" I didn't understand what he meant and he repeated, "My hands ... are black! They're burnt!" So, he was not merely an observer in this tragedy. He had also been injured, but had not noticed it until now due to the shock of what was happening. I gave Katie suggestions that she would experience no physical discomfort, although I have since been told by medical experts that this type of burn would be so deep that the nerve endings would be destroyed and there would be no pain, at least not immediately. I did not know this at the time and my only concern was for Katie's welfare.

D: *Are your hands the only part that looks black?*

K: No. My ... face feels as if there is nothing ... no skin. (He moaned.)

I had to push this revolting picture from my mind if I were to continue.

He asked in a voice like a little lost child, "What happens now ...? Where will I go ...? Maybe ... there are others like me, wandering around. I stumble ... and I fall. And I get up and I try again."

D: *Do you think you could find your way back to where you were living?*
K: It's gone. It's all gone. ... I must leave, but where should I go?
D: *Where are you trying to go?*
K: Away. Out. Any way to leave. To go away ... away from this ... horror.
D: *Where are the others going?*
K: The ones that I can see ... they are like me ... they are just ... stumbling, and ... they are lost.
D: *You know, you told me before that the planes came over every morning. Did you see any planes this morning?*
K: (As though just realizing there might be a connection.) Yes ... right ... right before this. Could they ...? They ... must have ... dropped ... some horrible ... *thing!* (Gasp) How could anyone *do* that? How? Don't they know what they have done? Do they care?

The words were like a forlorn voice crying in the wilderness.

D: *Do you think there is some connection between what has happened and the planes that went over?*
K: (He was upset.) That can be the only explanation. They must have ... *done* something! (His voice was filled with incredulity.) They've killed the town! A *whole* town! It's gone! (Suddenly he moaned.) I feel like my insides are on fire. Everything is ... it's ... as if ... someone struck a match and placed it inside of me, and it's become a bonfire. And it's ablaze!

I reacted quickly to give suggestions that she would feel no pain or discomfort. Experts have said Nogorigatu's lungs were probably burnt from breathing the incredibly hot wind. This often occurs when people breathe smoke from a fire. The feeling of pain could have been delayed due to the first shock reaction. This is pure speculation and his physical symptoms could have been caused by deep burns or the radiation or something we are not aware of.

Katie could have turned into an observer at any time and described the scenes to me, but apparently her subconscious wanted her to experience this. Or perhaps her own soul thought she needed to remember this in great detail. She was so wrapped up in this experience that she kept overriding my suggestions that she remain objective. I tried to get Nogorigatu's attention off himself and his physical condition, but I was unsuccessful.

D: *Is anything else happening to the city? (I was thinking of a fire or something similar.)*

K: Not ... that I can tell. I ... I ... don't know. I can't ... see ... anything. This is ... I ... I ... don't know. I just ...

D: *Why? Is there too much confusion or what?*

K: (Slowly) I ... can't ... see much ... at all.

D: *Do you think something has affected your eyes?*

Could this have been a delayed reaction from the explosion, or was he mentally blocking out what he did not wish to see?

K: I ... I ... don't know. All I know is ... is pain and confusion, and the *horror. WHY?!*

It was obvious he could not detach himself from the emotions of what was happening. I am no sadist; I had no wish to make him suffer just to obtain this vital story. I decided to remove Katie from the scene and take her forward about a week. By that time I thought the Japanese man should be dead and he could look back on that life from the spirit state and tell me more about it. I was mistaken.

K: (The voice was very soft.) I am ... in a building. They have ... people have come. They are caring for those of us that are dying.

So the old Japanese man was hardier than I had suspected. He had managed to survive a week, even with the burns and radiation poisoning. It also fit with Katie's spontaneous memories of his life. She felt he had not died immediately, but had lingered for about nine days afterward.

D: *Are there many people there?*

K: There are *hundreds* of people ... that are slowly dying. We know this. (He sounded as though he had come to terms with a hopeless situation.) ... They said that it was a bomb. The Americans. They dropped a bomb.

D: *Is it possible that one bomb could have done all that?*

K: I do not know how. (A whisper) ... I do not know how. All I know is death and pain ... is my companion. (His voice broke.) It seems horrible ... that anyone could conceive something so terrible. (Gasp)

D: *What about your daughters? Have you seen them anywhere?*

K: (His voice a painful whisper.) No, they are probably dead. My grandchildren! (He sobbed that word.) All dead. ... It is merciful to have died then, not to live on.

D: *Are there doctors or nurses?*

K: Yes, but they cannot do anything. (His voice was so full of despair.) They just ... try to give us something for the pain. I don't know what it is. It helps some, but ... not much ... not much.

D: *It sounds like they have made a building into a hospital.*

K: Yes. And all you hear is the cries ... and people dying. The *children!* (He again sobbed that word.) Everyone. ... They're just waiting for us ... we will all die.

I have heard it said that our planes dropped leaflets in advance to warn the people to flee the city. I wondered now if this was true.

D: *I have heard it said that the Americans tried to warn your people that this would happen. Have you heard anyone say anything like that?*

K: I don't know. I ... don't know. ... They cannot care. *How* could we get to such a point where anyone would want to do this? Even *think* of doing something like this? How could anyone?

It was very hard for him to speak and occasionally he gasped the words.

D: *I don't know. It is hard to understand. It is hard to believe that it could happen. Okay, I think it is time that we leave that scene. Leave that scene with all its pain and all its suffering and leave it in the past where it belongs. We are going to drift away from it.*

The change in Katie was immediate. Her body relaxed and the color returned to her face. It was as if I had flipped a switch.

D: *You are a very sensitive man and a very compassionate man and we don't want to bring any of that pain and suffering forward. We will leave it right in the past where it belongs. I wish to thank you very much for telling me about it and talking about it. Remember, what you have experienced is only a memory. It happened a long time ago. It won't bother you in any way mentally or physically. It will never, ever bother you again because now you understand where it comes from and where it belongs.*

I was filled with a deep, quiet sadness. Nogorigatu's death had been so traumatic, I could not bear to bring Katie up with that as the last memory in her subconscious mind. The change in her was evident and I knew she had passed through this ordeal unscathed and she would have no waking memory of the experience. But I felt it would be only decent and fair to take her to a happier time before awakening. I also felt I owed it to the old man I had come to know and respect. It was my farewell, my eulogy to him. Or was I doing it for myself? I will never know; I only knew I could not in good conscience bring her up to a waking state from such soul-searing despair.

D: *Let's go back to the year 1930; back to a happier time, a happier day.*

The voice immediately changed from the pain-racked moans of the dying Japanese and became younger and more vibrant.

K: I'm working on my pots. I have taken them out of the kiln and they are cooling.

What more fitting time to return to? A time when the world was still peaceful and he was working on his pots, something that always gave him much pride.

K: They are very beautiful. Each unique in their own way. I take care in my work. My love shows in every piece that I make.
D: *(I felt such compassion for this man.) You do good work and take pride in it. You sell them and people buy them, and that shows they are worth something.*

I relaxed and felt a calmness settle over the room. I knew everything would be all right. My Japanese friend would at last find the peace his reincarnated soul had yearned for. He had fulfilled the mission he had begun when the hidden memories had emerged in the mind of Katie. He had at last been vindicated. His death was not in vain.

D: *Where is the family?*
K: (She was smiling.) My sons are in the field and my wife is in the house working. And I am working on my ... work.
D: *And it is a happy day, isn't it? A happy memory.*
K: Yes, I am very pleased. Knowing that my own hands have created the thing of beauty is very satisfying.

I could again see the younger Nogorigatu secretly creating his beloved little animals in defiance of his father.

D: *You like to make the little figures too, don't you?*
K: (She smiled) Yes.
D: *The little animals. Ah, that is a very good thing to do because you have pride in that. And this is a happy day. Keep the happy memories. Don't linger on the bad times. Remember the happy days; don't you agree?*
K: Yes, they are what make the memories ripe, when you can look back on them and smile.
D: *Yes, think of the good times and the bad times will take care of themselves. That sounds like something you would say, doesn't it?*

My heart had gone out to him. I had felt his pain and his sorrow and it seemed only fair that I had been able to bring him full circle to the same place that I had found him, working on his pots. Thus I could leave him with the memory of a happier time before the world had gone crazy. I knew I would never have any rest until his story was put down on paper and told to the rest of the world. I have fulfilled my silent promise to him.

Later, I was to think of more questions about the bombing that I would have liked answered. But I also kept my promise to Katie. I said we would explore it one time only. We have never returned to it. *Dear God!* Once was enough!

I learned during later sessions that she had entered the spirit resting-place on the other side for a while after the traumatic death at Hiroshima. This is a special place that is reserved for deaths such as this. She felt she had gotten rid of a lot of karma by the lingering death she had experienced. She then attended the school on the spirit plane where the masters and teachers helped with the evaluation of that life. That was where she was when she was called for this assignment and the exchange of souls with the entity that had previously occupied Katie's body. (These states of being are explored further in my book, *Conversations with a Spirit.*)

When I met Katie the following week after experiencing the death of Nogorigatu, she said she felt terrific. A great weight had been lifted from her. She knew beyond a shadow of a doubt that the memory would ever bother her again. She was so estatic; we knew it had been worth all we had gone through together to obtain the story. She began to change after this experience. As we continued to work together, she began to mature rapidly.

Chapter 14

Research

*A*T LAST MY SESSIONS WERE FINISHED and I had completed my questioning about the life of the Japanese man. I had never before heard the story of the war presented from this point of view ... but was it true? It was a totally new way of looking at it. Were the people really having such a hard time finding food? Were they really oppressed by their own soldiers? Were the men taken forcibly into the army and the women taken to work in the factories? It was now time to begin my research to verify or disprove the events as Katie presented them in deep trance. This was the part I always enjoyed, for I deeply love delving into books and spending hours searching through a library for that one elusive bit of information.

When I began working with Katie, I did not know much about this event of history even though I was alive at the time it happened. The average person in those days only knew the story as the radio and newspapers presented it. Only those who had enough deep interest searched out and found more complete information. The bombing of Hiroshima did not personally touch us, except to announce the end of the war.

There was great rejoicing and happiness when the Japanese surrendered. It never occurred to anyone that others' suffering had brought about this celebration. So many of our own men had died, we considered this the end of a nightmare and America looked forward to the return to normalcy. We knew about the bombing, but it had no more personal connection than the war movies we had been bombarded with during that wartime period. Only later did the event begin to make the news again as the subject of radioactivity was understood and its deadly effects were studied. It was then labeled a black mark on our history. People wondered how we, as such a humane nation, could have done this horrible thing. The controversy stirred by this event has been reverberating down through time since that day in 1945.

These things did not become personal to me until I experienced it firsthand with Nogorigatu. Thus, when I began my research, I knew only the basic facts and the scantiest of information. I thought it would be a simple matter to investigate because it was such a recent historical event. All I had to do was find accounts of the war and the bombing and see if Nogorigatu's story matched what others had reported.

Instead, I found that very little research has ever been conducted by Japan or the u.s. into the experiences of the *people* on the day the bomb was dropped or the after-effects they suffered. There has been a great deal written on the moral implications of our actions—about the manufacture and experimentation of the bomb and the pros and cons between our own government and the scientists during the time preceding the bombing. Also much on the flight of the "Enola Gay," the b-29 that dropped the bomb, and Commander Tibbetts, the pilot of the plane. But precious little has been written about the people and what they experienced, unless it was done from a clinical and textbook point of view with all emotions removed. There are the books, *Hiroshima* by John Hersey and *Hiroshima Diary* by M. Hachiya which are based on personal experiences. These have become classics and are source books for anyone doing research in this complicated subject.

Many research projects were begun shortly after the war, but were abandoned when the enormity of the horror of the event began to unfold. The researchers were human, after all. The book, *Death in Life* by Robert J. Lifton is unique because it was the first time a psychiatrist studied the emotional effects on survivors and it was written 20 years after the event. He found the people were reluctant to talk to Americans because they were afraid we would use any information to make bigger and better weapons.

The author of this book reported that he could understand the reluctance of other investigators to complete their projects because he finally had to seal himself off emotionally from the tales of horror he heard. It was the only way he could remain objective and collect information. This was the same problem I had; you have to keep from being caught up and becoming involved in the story. This could be compared to other equally emotionally charged events of the war, such as the Jewish Holocaust. These are things that revolt and repulse the human soul. There has been a campaign in recent years to deny that the Holocaust ever happened. The same thing has happened, to a lesser degree, with the atom bomb. They cannot deny that it happened, so it is played down and hushed up. Maybe humans do not like to think they are really capable of such depths of horror and inhumanity to their fellow creatures.

My research disclosed an amazing amount of accuracy, as Katie's account proved correct point by point. I still get cold shivers when I come across a piece of information (no matter how small) that verifies something from a hypnotic regression. The story began to emerge. The Emperor had not wanted the war, it was the military regime of the country that brought this about. I see him as similar to the Queen of England, a mere figurehead, while the government was actually run by the Cabinet or Diet. This was as Nogorigatu said, that it was a general who made the power-hungry decision. Once the war began Japan became a country fanatical about winning. Even when the Japanese people began to suffer, the military would not give in. The leaders tried to convince the people that, if they would hang in there, everything would work out.

The blockades, bombings and disruptions of supply and trade routes were having their effect upon the country. Toward the end of the war, even the students in the schools and colleges were put into forced labor to help with the war effort. The necessity for more airplanes, in particular, was the goal of the government. They were being defeated because of the lack of air cover. The supply ships couldn't get through to the island bases without airplanes for protection. Thus the people were spurred on to make more planes and guns and war supplies and forget about food and clothing production. The government believed if only they could produce more airplanes they would win the war. But then the disruption of supply routes and our bombing of train lines created more problems. The raw materials couldn't be brought to the factories.

It is a fact there were many factories in Hiroshima—this was one main reason for considering it as a bomb target. These factories were working hard, trying to turn out supplies and equipment for the Army to defend their homeland in case of attack. The average person did not know about the dwindling supplies of raw materials in those last days. The city had been a major debarkation point for troops and a major shipping port.

Now the only troops in Hiroshima were for defense of the city and the once-busy harbor was dead because American planes had dropped so many mines into the offshore waters.

There was a strict wartime censorship that kept most of the news of the war from the people. It is also true that there were food shortages and diminishing food rations in Hiroshima in those last days before the bomb was dropped. Black markets were actively flourishing during this time period. They cropped up to deal with the bartering of items for needed foods and necessities. "Things" were more important (as Nogorigatu said) and open trade was the only way of obtaining anything other than the basic essentials. Money was being hoarded away for later, when it would again regain its value. Rice was Japan's biggest crop, but it became so costly that some of the peasant growers could not afford to eat it. As we have seen from our story, many of the farmers were not allowed to grow it through gross mismanagement. Japan was importing extra food supplies from occupied Thailand and French Indochina and these supply routes were cut off by the u.s. Navy blockade during those months in 1945.

It was a fact that there was a tightening food situation in the city and the number of food retailers had dwindled drastically. Quote from *No High Ground,* by F. Knebel and C.W. Bailey ii:

> "The average citizen might know only that his rice ration was smaller or that the corner grocery store had gone out of business because it had little or nothing to sell. But the Japanese cabinet knew more. An official study in June had predicted that minimum requirements for rice to support the people on a subsistence-only basis would outrun supplies by a full 14 million tons in 1945. It added that the first grim signs of starvation were already beginning to appear in more isolated sections of Japan."

Nogorigatu's farm could have been located in such a section.

When the Americans entered Japan as an occupation force, they found the people reduced almost to a starvation diet. It seemed that the black picture Nogorigatu had painted about the conditions of his country were true; he had not exaggerated. The country was indeed falling apart internally, starving and spurred on by false hopes of victory.

Since nothing like the atomic bomb had ever occurred in the history of humankind, there was nothing that could prepare the people of Hiroshima for what was to come. They naturally expected conventional bombing because it was happening all over their country. Nogorigatu said they watched the bombers going over and wondered, not "if," but "when."

The military authorities were also worried and, fearing attack might come at any time, ordered houses destroyed to create firebreaks and firelanes throughout the city. The army ordered the people drafted into labor battalions to do this work. Women and older school children were assigned in large groups for the tearing down of houses. They were ordered to destroy almost 70,000 dwellings in hopes of saving the city in case of incendiary bombings similar to those that had been occurring throughout Japan. All able-bodied girls in the secondary schools were ordered to join this "volunteer" work group and boys were drafted for labor in the city's factories. Many lived in dormitories at the factories and classes were held each day before the students went to work. These are examples of people being forcibly put to work, such as Nogorigatu described. It is not too far-fetched to believe that it was true that his daughters-in-law were also made to work in the factories against their will. This seemed to be the existing pattern.

Because of the destruction of homes to create the firebreaks and firelanes, over 90,000 people had been ordered to leave in five mass evacuations. But from our story we can see this worked both ways; others may have been coming into the city to find food and work. The authorities became concerned about the flow of unauthorized evacuees and by the middle of the summer soldiers were manning the major exit roads and turning back those whose departure had not been approved by the authorities. This would explain why Nogorigatu was no longer able to journey back and forth to his farm about that time. He also spoke of people being stopped on the streets and questioned. He said there was a lot of tension and suspicion around that time.

The authorities knew Hiroshima's turn would surely come and they wanted to be prepared. Of course, they had no way of knowing there was no possible preparation for what was to come.

While almost every other urban area in Japan had been seared by the incendiary fire-bombs dropped by the B-29s, Hiroshima had been strangely spared. There had been only 12 enemy missiles in 3½ years of war. Two small bombs were dropped by a flight of U.S. Navy Raiders in March 1945 and six weeks later a single B-29, unable to reach its prime target, dropped ten bombs on an outlying area. In these incidents about a dozen people were killed.

Amazingly these facts are identical with what Nogorigatu said when I questioned him in July, 1945. He said, "They've had bombings around the city ... two of the outlying factories have been hit. No serious damage, some deaths." Thus enemy planes flew overhead night and day, causing continual air-raid alarms, but they went on elsewhere. Hiroshima seemed to be forgotten.

When the people gradually realized that their city was one of the few major cities left in Japan that had not been badly bombed, many strange and often humorous rumors circulated to try to explain why the city was being spared. Many of these were far-fetched but they only served to illustrate how concerned the confused people were for an explanation. Many tried to ignore it and go on about their lives, but others knew something was wrong and they felt the feeling of impending doom while wondering what the Americans were planning for them. Many knew the situation was not natural and they joked that maybe Hiroshima was not on the American maps.

Quote from *Death in Life:*

> "Many used the Japanese word 'bukimi,' meaning weird, ghastly, or unearthly, to describe Hiroshima's uneasy combination of continued good fortune and expectation of catastrophe. People remembered saying to one another, 'Will it be tomorrow or the day after tomorrow?' "

This was the atmosphere Nogorigatu described. Another quote from *No High Ground:*

> "There were those in Hiroshima, describing themselves as 'intellectuals,' who feared, as they lay awake at night listening to the planes overhead, that the Yankees were saving them for some particularly dreadful fate."

They could not have imagined at that time the macabre reason behind their good fortune.

American intelligence officers agreed that to make the maximum imprint on the Japanese government the atomic bomb should explode over a relatively untouched city. There were not many left to choose from since our conventional bombings had already reduced hundreds of square miles of metropolitan Japan to rubble. Hiroshima was one of the sites chosen and was ordered omitted from regular bombing raids in preparation for the A-bomb test.

So far the city had been untouched and the air-raid alerts had become so frequent that the people were lulled into a false sense of security. They no longer fled to the safety of the air raid shelters every time the alarm sounded. This was a case of "crying wolf once too often." It was true as Nogorigatu said, the people had become so accustomed to it they could set their clocks by the planes that went over at the same time every morning. These were actually weather planes that preceded the bombers. Their job was to radio the weather conditions and direct the bombers to the best targets. And Hiroshima had not been on the list until that fateful day.

I also discovered that although leaflets were dropped over Japan warning the people of conventional bombing raids, Hiroshima was not warned of the impending atomic bombing in any way. It was the best-kept secret of the war.

There had been two alerts during the wee morning hours of August 6, 1945, that had kept residents running to and from the shelters. Was it any wonder the majority ignored the alarms and tried to go on about their daily lives? After having been up twice during the night with the other two alarms, most people paid little attention to the alert around 7:00 A.M. It was a single B-29 flying very high. It seemed to be the same type of plane they had become so accustomed to seeing flying over at that time of the morning. It crossed the city twice and then flew out to sea and the all-clear sounded around 7:30. They could not know that this plane was the "Straight Flush," the weather plane that was preceding the "Enola Gay," the bomber that was to drop the world's first atomic bomb. It is a matter of record that no alert was sounded when Tibbets' plane flew over the city shortly afterwards around 8:00 A.M. The all-clear had been sounded only a half-hour before, thus the city was experiencing the equivalent of an early morning "rush-hour" with the majority of its people outside when the bomb was dropped.

The bomb exploded completely on target with the force equivalent of 20,000 tons of TNT, with a temperature at the center of the fireball of 1,000,000°F., 1800 feet in the air near the center of a flat city built mainly of wood. It was as if a piece of the sun had reached out with its incredible heat and touched the Earth.

In the book, *No High Ground,* the author gives a very good illustration of the city of Hiroshima. It was a city of many rivers and bridges (as Nogorigatu so accurately described) and the city was located on the pieces of land between these bridges. The author compared it to stretching out the five fingers of your left hand—this was the way the city was laid out—with the fingers representing the city and the spaces representing the rivers that flowed into the sea. Where the wedding ring would normally be worn on that hand would represent where the bomb center or epicenter was located. The epicenter (sometimes called hypocenter) could be determined by the type of destruction. The giant stone pillars flanking the entrance of the Shima Surgical Hospital were rammed straight down into the ground from the force of the blast and thus this spot was later declared to have been at the center. If the epicenter had been to either side of this building, the columns would have been blown over, not driven straight down.

The sequence of events described by survivors who were further out from the center were: A blinding flash of light and at the same moment the feeling of burning heat. Then a few seconds later a huge "boom," and a violent rush of air followed by shattering noises. Then they saw an enormous mass of clouds which spread and climbed rapidly into the sky. There it hung horizontally and took on the shape of a monstrous mushroom with the lower part as its stem, or as one person described it, "the tail of a tornado."

The survivors later devised a nickname for the bomb and the event: "pikadon." This means "flash-boom," and was their definition of what happened, according to where the people were when the explosion occurred. Some closer to the epocenter remembered only the flash of light, or "pika." Those further away saw the flash and also heard the loud boom or "don." Thus according to where they were when the bomb fell they speak of the "pika" or the "pikadon."

This all fits Nogorigatu's description of the sequence of events with remarkable accuracy. He was in the market when the bomb fell, a place that held many happy memories for him. Habit, familiarity and perhaps a longing for his old way of life probably drew him there. Since he both saw the flash and heard the boom, this was verification that he was a distance away from the blast. He said the marketplace was located on the southern edge of the city where one of the highways entered. Maps show this to have been a few miles from the epocenter.

The effects of this bomb were so startling it is mind-boggling and almost impossible to comprehend. First came the heat which turned the central part of the city into a gigantic oven. It lasted only an instant but was so intense it melted metal, stone and roof tiles. It literally incinerated every human being near the epocenter so completely that nothing remained except their shadows burned forever into asphalt pavements or stone walls. This was another method of determining where the epocenter was located, by measuring the slant of these shadows. This would have been at ground zero but beyond that point, many deaths occurred from severe burns. Bare skin was burned up to 2½ miles away. The patterns of people's clothing was burned and etched into their skin by the heat. Those caught outside in the open were severely burned because they had nothing to block the rays. This would have been what happened to Nogorigatu. Our Japanese friend said he was outside, unsheltered, in the open marketplace. According to the injuries he received and the fact that he did not die immediately, this would have been completely correct with his distance from the epocenter. Many other people who were not directly exposed and apparently not injured at all, later died from the radiation sickness that destroyed their white blood cells.

Immediately after the heat came the blast, sweeping outward from the fireball with the forces of a *500-mile-per-hour* wind. This amount of force is incomprehensible to our human mind. It could be compared to about five times the destructive power of a normal hurricane. There was an area of complete, total annihilation for about two miles in all directions. Virtually all the buildings were destroyed within a three-mile radius in all directions or roughly the entire city limits. Thousands were killed instantly from flying debris and collapsing buildings. Those further out from the epocenter who were sheltered in reinforced concrete buildings had the most protection. The only things left standing were a few office buildings that had been specially built to resist earthquakes, but their roofs were driven down and the interiors destroyed. Other things that did not offer any resistance, such as bridges, utility poles, etc. were left standing. So quickly did the blast follow the heat that for many they seemed to come together.

Fires began instantly in thousands of places at once, thus the fire-breaks the city had prepared were useless. Between the blast and the fire every single building within an area of almost five square miles around the zero point were destroyed. Only the skeletons of strong, concrete and steel buildings were left standing.

Then came the strange black rain, a frightening phenomenon resulting from the vaporization of moisture in the fireball and condensation in the cloud that spouted up from it. It did not help put out the fires but only served to further confuse and frighten the people. Next a huge black cloud of dust descended upon the city obliterating the sun and turning the day into night. Along with the possible psychological reason for Nogorigatu not being able to see, this unexplained sudden darkness could have added to the confusion, and coupled with the other factors, made him temporarily blind.

After the rain came a wind—the great "fire-wind"—which blew back in toward the center of the catastrophe, increasing in force as the air over Hiroshima grew hotter and hotter because of the great fires. The wind was strong enough to uproot large trees. Was this the wind Nogorigatu spoke of or the first wind that followed the blast? We have no idea of how much time elapsed in his account of the event.

Quote from *Hiroshima and Nagasaki Reconsidered* by Barton J. Bernstein:

"According to a British study, eyewitnesses agreed that they saw a blinding white flash in the sky, felt a rush of air and heard a loud rumble of noise, followed by the sound of rending and the falling of buildings. All spoke of the settling darkness as they found themselves enveloped by a universal cloud of dust. Men, women and children were torn in pieces, and the smell of burned flesh and the *memory of agonized cries lingered*. Others died from radiation, some quickly, some slowly. Most of the industrial workers had already reported to work, but many workers were en route and nearly all the school children and some industrial employees were at work in the open." (Italics mine.)

Survivors have described their shock upon looking toward the center of the city after smoke and dust cleared and finding it had completely disappeared, wiped out in an instant. Even observers who later flew over the area remarked about this strange total devastation, unlike anything they had ever seen before in wartime bombing. Quote from a survivor:

"I saw that Hiroshima had disappeared ... I was shocked by the sight ... What I felt then and still feel now I just can't explain with words. Seeing nothing left of Hiroshima was so shocking that I simply can't express what I felt ... I could see a few buildings standing, but Hiroshima didn't exist—that was mainly what I saw—Hiroshima just didn't exist."

A quote from Dr. Hachiya's *Hiroshima Diary*:

"For acres and acres the city was like a desert except for scattered piles of brick and roof tiles. I had to revise my meaning of the word destruction or choose some other word to describe what I saw. Devastation may be a better word, but really, I know of no word or words to describe the view."

The dominant theme repeated by the survivors was the over-powering feelings of confusion, helplessness and abandonment. Nogorigatu felt all these emotions. One man interviewed by Lifton said, "The feeling I had was that everyone was dead. The whole city was destroyed. I thought this was the end of Hiroshima ... of Japan ... of humankind." The feeling was that the whole world was dying, a complete immersion in death.

These statements sound very much like those expressed by our Japanese friend. His emotions and observations agree amazingly with the facts. I cannot help but conclude Katie had to have actually been there as a participant to report in such astonishing detail. These are details that I believe are known by a small minority of people. Only those interested would ever have come across them, certainly not a young girl with little formal education. To her the idea of even think-ing about it was appalling, so it was very doubtful she would have done any independent research. This will undoubtedly be raised as a pos-sibility, but it is a possibility I will not accept because I was later to take her through 26 lives and I found this incredible ability for detail repeated time and again. At that time she was more interested in finding the cause of her involuntary memories and fears. I know she had neither the time nor the inclination to resort to the difficult type of research that I must do when investigating this type of phenomenon.

The number of deaths, immediately and over a period of time, will probably never be known and is even today disputed. The Americans have always said there were about 70,000 killed but the Japanese disagree. They claim that the Americans have always intentionally kept the figures lower than the actual ones. The Japanese claim that the city was more congested than we realized and that 60 percent of the population was within 1.2 miles of the epocenter. Population could have been greater when you think of Nogorigatu's circum-stances multiplied many times, people coming to the city to escape hunger and oppression in the rural areas. Hiroshima estimates the figures were closer to 200,000 or roughly 50 percent of the city's day-time population (also a disputed figure, varying from 227,000 to over 400,000) killed by the bomb. These would have included people coming in from outlying areas to work, people who did not normally live within the city limits. Many other Japanese sources think it was around 100,000 killed. It has been said the destruction was so widespread that all of Hiroshima immediately became involved. There are so many factors to be considered that it is agreed that no one will ever know the true figures and the controversy continues to the present day.

Our experts had predicted lower casualty rates because they thought the people would use the air-raid shelters. Also the scientists had not expected the radiation to reach the ground in such deadly doses. The bomb's damage was much greater than anyone could have imagined.

Nogorigatu said people were wandering about with their arms held out. They didn't know where they were going; they just wanted to get out, away from the horror. This was true. After the explosion, thousands of people were simply fleeing blindly and without any objective except to get out of the city. Many were pushed off the bridges by the crush of fleeing humanity and drowned in the rivers.

This fact was observed by many who were coming into the city to see what had happened. They spoke of the lines of people wandering from the city. They were so severely burned their skin was blackened. They were said to resemble Negroes more than Japanese. They walked with their badly burnt arms bent forward, held out so as not to touch their bodies. Their hair was completely burnt off. Depending upon the severity of the burns, many had no outer layer of skin at all, even the skin of their faces had dropped off like a mask. On others, their skin on their hands, faces and bodies hung down in strips and pieces. This was what Nogorigatu said of his own condition, his hands were black and he felt he had no skin on his face. People fitting this description were everywhere and many of them died alongside the road. Many other observations from survivors implied that these victims no longer appeared human. Many, many others walked very slowly trying to get out of the city. They were described as "walking ghosts," and "automatons walking in the realm of dreams," so complete was their shock and disassociation with reality. It has been said that it would be unbelievable for people burned so badly to have even moved, let alone walked. Maybe the shock was so great it made things happen that were impossible under normal conditions.

Since most of the existing hospitals, doctors and medical personnel were destroyed in the explosion, it was very difficult to find a place to take the wounded. Some makeshift hospitals sprung up within the burned-out shells of buildings, as in *Hiroshima Diary*. Others were set up in buildings further from the blast that had survived more or less intact. Medical supplies were almost nonexistent and the few doctors and nurses that had survived performed miracles in the limited care they could give. Only 28 doctors were left alive and able to work in this large city where half the people were casualties. The sick and dying were crowded into every available space, but proper care could not be given because of the lack of supplies, training and sanitation facilities. Nothing like this had ever happened before in the history of humanity and doctors had no idea what they were fighting. All they could do was try to make the patients comfortable and treat their symptoms—an impossible situation due to the overcrowding and horrible sanitary conditions. *Hiroshima Diary* gives a very impressive account of this situation. The medical personnel were as confused and frightened as the victims.

It is unknown what really killed Nogorigatu. I was surprised he had not died immediately. There were probably a number of factors involved. The first initial deep burns were undoubtedly complicated by a strange symptom that appeared later in the makeshift hospitals: the destruction of the white blood cells in the body caused by the effects of the radiation. This caused the victims to hemorrhage from various parts of their bodies. There were also many symptoms caused by the "radiation sickness": vomiting, diarrhea and fever. Many victims lingered for a while enduring these different painful complications and eventually died.

I wish I could have asked Nogorigatu more questions later, after I had regained my composure. But I had to respect my promise to Katie that we would not return to that scene again. I especially wondered what happened to the bodies. I found out later through research that the bodies were cremated in huge piles. The Japanese normally cremate their dead anyway, but this was done for a different reason: to control the spread of disease. Since there was no time for religious ceremony, the average Japanese thought this form of disposal was terribly disrespectful to the dead and went strictly against their religious beliefs. But they came to realize there was no other solution. They became, however reluctant, accustomed to the stench of burning bodies that soon hung like a pall over the demolished city. The care of the sick and the survival of the living became much more important than the reverent disposal of the dead. For the survivors, it became a living nightmare from which many have never awakened, as the effects of radiation are still being seen today, passed on through the genes to later generations.

Chapter 15

The Finale

I HAD ONCE MORE GONE THROUGH TIME to experience history as it was being made. I had seen, through the eyes of an eyewitness, one the most horrendous events in our recent time. Was Katie really there? Did she actually live the life of the Japanese man that she described in such astonishing detail? It appears to be so, when you remember the trauma she felt as the original memory was triggered and brought to the surface, and the extreme relief and happiness when it was over. Where else could these memories have come from? Surely not from her conscious mind and certainly not from mine.

If a modern young girl were going to fantasize and invent a past life, it would be logical to assume she would pick one about romance and excitement, not one about such absolute horror.

Those who do not believe in reincarnation will have other explanations for this strange phenomenon. But does it really matter? The important thing is that it helped Katie; she has grown much from the experience. It is also important that we are at last able to see the war from a different viewpoint. Of course, this was the view of one individual living at that time. Others may have had different opinions. I was alive during that war and, as a child growing up then, I know my remembrances are different from an adult's or someone who fought in the war. Does this make it any less true? We all see things from within our own reality.

Our propaganda at the time had convinced us the Japanese were terrible monsters without souls. They were the enemy and, at that time, we were so conditioned we would not have even considered that the everyday people in that country could be any different from us:

confused and frightened. We thought they were monsters and they thought we were monsters. But in reality no one was a monster and yet everyone was.

Nogorigatu gives us a poignant story of the helplessness of the average Japanese caught up in a war situation they did not want or understand. Like people everywhere, they only wanted their lives to continue as they had in the past. The military elements of the government were the ones that wanted power and influence in the world. This story points up the very real fact that governments, not people, make wars. The innocent are the ones that suffer the most, losing their homes and their families in the insanity that prevails. They are often the pawns of the powerful, but if left up to the individual, there would be no wars. I believe from this story that these are the feelings of the average person anywhere in the world.

There are still those who say that since Japan started the war, through their bombing of Pearl Harbor, they deserved anything that happened to them. But who are "they"? Through this regression "they" are stripped of their cloak of invisibility. "They" become human beings, people. "They" are Nogorigatu, his wife, his sons and their grandchildren. Herein lies the injustice of war since time began.

I thought long and hard about writing this book. If few others had wanted to investigate the bomb, did I really want to open that "can of worms"? Did I really want to hold up a mirror and make man take a long, hard look at himself? Maybe it would be better to "let the sleeping giant lie." But maybe this is the reason behind this story— to open that can, through this unusual approach, and place it on our doorstep—to take a look inside and make sure it will never happen again.

The controversy will undoubtedly continue down through history as to whether we did the right thing or not, whether we took all the factors into consideration. The entire issue is very complex. After five years of fighting all over the world, we wanted the war to be over and our men returned home to try to reassemble their war-torn lives.

We could not sympathize with the enemy. Enemies must be clearly defined in order for people to fight a war and kill each other. War could not exist any other way. They must be anonymous villains or heartless monsters. If you come to know the man as a person, you cannot fight him. Nogorigatu put this very well in his story.

I had no idea when I began that I was to uncover an even more powerful story that was linked directly with the life of Nogorigatu. If I had not begun researching the bombing of Hiroshima to verify Katie's regression, I would not have uncovered the deeper story. Maybe it is not always a good idea to journey backwards in time and see the truth about history, because then we may have to face the harsh reality of what really happened, and it isn't always the easiest thing to look at. I know I cannot sit in judgment because I am only a "recorder," a "researcher," and I feel a moral obligation to put down what I have uncovered. Let others sort out the reasons and purposes.

The information is available to anyone who cares to do the research. It is not hidden. Maybe others have tried to tell the true story, but we have been too preoccupied to listen. I know it never had meaning to me until Katie relived it so vividly through Nogorigatu's memories.

The unpopularity of the war with the Japanese people was evident when Nogorigatu spoke of the soldiers being stationed throughout the countryside to keep the "dissidents" in line. The government must have been very much afraid that a revolution or civil war would be created by the unrest and unhappiness of their people. If anyone spoke out, they were killed. This was the easiest way to stop rebellion before it began. Also, the people were starving to death and money had lost its value. It has been reported by newspapers that Japan was prepared to fight to the last man to protect its Emperor and homeland. I do not believe this. The people were too concerned with just staying alive. They may have fought to protect their own families, but I think mass confusion would have been the result. Nogorigatu said he considered the real enemy to be the government and the soldiers; they were the ones who had caused him such grief.

Which brings us to the question, "Did we really need to drop the A-bomb?" It is my belief, from what I learned with this regression, that the atomic bomb was not needed. Japan was falling apart internally and could not have held out much longer. But some people have said, "How could our government have known about conditions existing within Japan?" Did we have spies within the country that reported back to Washington? Before I began my research I didn't know, but, to give our government the benefit of a doubt, I liked to think maybe they didn't know what was really happening.

What I found in my research left me with a very bitter taste. We *did* know of the conditions within Japan—that she was on her knees. We *knew* Japan was trying to surrender in the summer of 1945. But because of many diverse and complex political reasons, we decided to use the bomb anyway.

This is still the greatest country in the world, but we are only as good as our leaders. They are only human, and being human, are capable of error. In 1939, President Roosevelt was approached by scientists who had escaped from Europe. They told him they feared Germany might be developing atomic weapons. Before this time, the Navy had experimented somewhat with atoms, but in 1939 the President told the scientists to begin research. At that time, we were supposedly a peaceful country trying to remain isolated from the war clouds that were growing in Europe. In October, 1941, the President decided to endorse an "all-out" research project to investigate the possibilities of atomic energy for military purposes. The weapon to be invented was primarily intended to be used against Germany. The project was begun in deepest secrecy and was perhaps the best kept secret of our time. Only a handful of men in the United States ever knew what was happening. The money to finance the research came from special hidden funds so that not even Congress had an inkling of what was being developed. Roosevelt was in constant contact with the scientists throughout the project and followed their work through six years. Before it was developed, the bomb was to cost a staggering $2 billion dollars, an enormous amount of money before our inflationary times.

Roosevelt never fully trusted the Soviets and believed, in late 1942, that the bomb could play a critical role in dealing with them—both as a military weapon in war and as a diplomatic weapon in peace. For this reason he did not tell the Soviets anything about the research, although England's Churchill knew.

However, Roosevelt was not to live to see the final results of the experiment he had started. He died of a brain hemorrhage in April, 1945, and Vice-President Harry S Truman became President. An hour after he was sworn in, Truman was told for the first time of the awesome responsibility that was to be his. I wonder how he felt, having just become President under unfavorable circumstances and then suddenly thrust into such a position. He knew he had inherited the responsibility of ending the war, but prior to this time Truman had no inkling of atomic research.

Roosevelt had several years to come to his decision and plan his strategy about the bomb. He had the terrible responsibility of making these grave wartime decisions with no historical examples or past experiences to guide him. Maybe these problems hastened his death. Truman had the whole thing dropped in his lap and had only a few months to assimilate the awful implications of his impending decision. He would have to rely solely on the advice of others. When it comes down to it, the President has the least amount of freedom of any American citizen. His opinions are governed by the advice of many other people. But in the final judgment, the President alone must have the last word. Truman always said, "The buck stops here." Did he make the right decision? Would any of us have acted differently if we had been thrust suddenly into such an unenviable position?

The main concern was not Germany or Japan. Truman was told that our possessing and demonstrating the bomb would make the Soviets more manageable in the future.

After Truman had been briefed on the atomic problem, Secretary of War Henry Stimson urged him to appoint a committee to advise him. There was much discussion about how America's use of the revolutionary weapon would appear to future generations. There was also discussion about whether the use of the bomb could be avoided. Some scientists hoped the research would be fruitless. But Roosevelt had set the project in motion and Truman never questioned the fact that he must continue the legacy. He accepted what Roosevelt's advisors told him. All the plans were in progress and all details had been worked out. All Truman had to do was carry them out. Could it be that, after so many years of secretive experiments, the government did not want to see their work go down the drain without testing the final result? As the bomb neared completion, the war in Europe was coming to a halt, finally ending with VE (Victory in Europe) Day on May 8, 1945. Time was running out. There was only one place left to try the expensive experiment, but they had to hurry before the war in Japan could end as well. Where would they ever get the chance to prove the bomb once the war ended? There might never be such a golden opportunity again. Was the bomb a final test of a scientific experiment with the Japanese used as unfortunate guinea pigs? Was Truman so fearful of the mounting threat from the Russians that he wanted to show them what a powerful weapon we had in order to subdue them?

For humane reasons, the scientists on the committee suggested the possibility of demonstrating the bomb before foreign observers. Would such a demonstration of the bomb's power persuade the Japanese to surrender? Another suggestion was to warn the Japanese of the incredible potential of the new weapon and then drop it only if they did not surrender within a certain number of days. Would warnings and invitations to see a demonstration be enough? The world had nothing to compare this with; they would surely think it was only propaganda and ignore it. If this happened we would lose the shock value of the bomb.

Unaware of the atomic research being conducted, military advisors continued developing their long-range plans for ending the war with Japan. Now that the war was over in Europe, they could turn all their attention to the war in the Pacific. They conceived Project OLYMPIC, the first land assault on the Japanese mainland. Their plans included the use of 42 aircraft carriers, 24 battleships, 212 destroyers and 183 destroyer escorts. Six divisions of infantry would go ashore on D-Day, with three more following on the next day. Four more divisions would be in reserve. In all, three quarter million men would be involved. Twelve hospital ships would be offshore and could evacuate 30,000 wounded to waiting hospitals in the Philippines, the Marianas and Okinawa where 54,000 beds were to be ready. It was clear that they were expecting to meet great opposition. There was to be an LST (landing ship tank) loaded with whole blood at each beachhead. It was thought the Japanese had probably fixed heavy artillery positions to cover all proposed landing beaches and had laid minefields. We expected to meet defenses and tactics of the type encountered in Okinawa where many American lives were lost.

The military strategy was to first intensify the aerial bombing of

Japan. Second, if Japan had not surrendered by November, 1945, they would begin OLYMPIC on the southern end of Japan. This was to be followed in the spring of 1946 by the landing on the Tokyo plain. These were the plans Truman intended to use if the A-bomb was not developed before that time, or if something went wrong with the experiment.

In March, 1945, Japan was beginning to be subjected to the mass bombardment of civilians, which had become commonplace in Europe during World War II. On March 9, 2,000 tons of incendiary bombs were dropped on Tokyo from planes flying as low as 5,000 feet, setting the city on fire. On that day, 78,000 Japanese were killed. With such bombing of cities accepted as common warfare, it was difficult for some military leaders to believe that a new weapon of destruction would be any more unethical than TNT and fire bombs. They saw Japan as a nation already wrecked and surrounded.

Preparations for OLYMPIC were going ahead and time was running out for those in Washington who wanted to see peace without an invasion of Japan. Truman wanted to make absolutely sure there was no alternative before ordering OLYMPIC. He did not want to order an invasion which might result in several hundred thousand American casualties if there was any other way out. Secretary of War Stimson, after conferring with other experts, reported that Japan could be made to surrender without invasion, thanks to air and sea bombardment and the naval blockage already under way. He thought these could be intensified and he knew we had a new secret weapon in our pocket that should be ready soon. Stimson was afraid that, if we landed in Japan, there would be great loss of life because Japan was prepared to fight to the last man. The President wondered whether the bomb had a chance of ending the war quickly, preventing further loss of American lives.

Although the public did not know it, there were many pro's and con's about the use of the bomb during this period. Hap Arnold, head of the Army Air Force, was convinced we were winning with conventional bombing raids on Japan. His advisors believed the bombing, coupled with the blockade, had brought the empire to its knees. Japan was short of gas and oil and most of her factories had been destroyed. Arnold did not believe the OLYMPIC invasion would be necessary. He also did not believe the explosion of the bomb was necessary to win the war.

On July 12, a poll of 150 scientists was taken at the Chicago Met Lab on how the bomb should be used. The majority elected to give a military demonstration in a remote area of Japan with an opportunity to surrender before the full use of the weapon was employed. Many others wanted a demonstration in an isolated area, New Mexico or an uninhabited island, with representatives from Japan present. However, these scientific discussions and reservations had little impact on the top-policy level. None of these alternatives seemed realistic and feasible, so the advisory committee's final report suggested that the bomb be dropped on Japan as soon as possible, without specific warning. Truman went along with this. It has been said that he wanted no warning given because the Japanese gave us no warning, and this was to be his revenge for the sneak attack at Pearl Harbor, as well as discipline for the bad treatment of our war prisoners. The committee suggested a target comprising a military installation and surrounding houses and buildings to show the maximum blast damage. They fully realized that many civilians would be killed and Truman said he had reached the same conclusion, but decided to proceed, provided the Japanese did not surrender and the first New Mexico test of the bomb proved successful.

Next, intelligence officers began work on target charts. The choice was limited. They all agreed that, to make the maximum imprint, the atomic bomb should explode over a relatively untouched city. The bombings by the B-29s had already reduced hundreds of square miles of metropolitan Japan to rubble. There had already been so much damage; it was feared the A-bomb would not have a fair background against which to show its strength. This was considered imperative to convince the Japanese government of the severity of the situation. It was also important to make an impression of our military strength on Russia. Hiroshima was one of the few untouched cities left, so it was a logical choice. It was also believed to be the only major city in Japan that did not have a prisoner of war camp. All the other cities on the list had sustained damage, except Kokura which had as many as four POW camps. Kyoto was removed from the list after much urging because of its many religious shrines. When the list was approved, the possible targets were ordered omitted from regular bombing raids in preparation for the test.

Leaflets were dropped over Japan during this time period, listing many Japanese cities to be bombed. The following is the text of these leaflets:

"Attention Japanese people: Read this carefully, as it may save your life or the life of a relative or friend.

"In the next few days the military installations in four or more of the cities named on the reverse side will be destroyed by American bombs. These cities contain military installations and workshops or factories which produce military goods.

"We are determined to destroy all of the tools of the military clique which they are using to prolong this useless war. But unfortunately bombs have no eyes. So, in accordance with America's well known humanitarian policies, the American Air Force, which does not wish to injure innocent people, now gives you warning to evacuate the cities named and save your lives.

"America is not fighting the Japanese people but is fighting the military clique which has enslaved the Japanese people. The peace which America will bring will free the people from the oppression of the military clique and mean the emergence of a new and better Japan.

"You can restore peace by demanding new and good leaders who will end the war.

"We cannot promise that only these cities will be among those attacked, but at least four will be, so heed this warning and evacuate these cities immediately."

Hiroshima was *not* one of the cities mentioned in the leaflets.

This was an unprecedented move on our part. It was something that had never been done by any country during wartime. The move was criticized by some military leaders who said it would make our planes "sitting ducks." But instead, when the B-29s bombed Tokyo and other large cities with incendiary bombs they met no opposition at all. No planes were sent aloft and there was very little anti-aircraft fire. Nogorigatu had said it was almost a game, as though the anti-aircraft gunners were not even trying to hit the planes, just firing a few shots and quitting. Even if the enemy thought the leaflets were propaganda at first, when the bombings became reality, you would think they would have taken the warnings seriously. We were burning and destroying whole cities with little opposition. It was eerie, but I believe it showed a doomed and dying country on its last legs. We now know that there was a great shortage of ammunition in the country. From *No High Ground:*

> "Japan, desperately short of war supplies, wasted no fuel or ammunition on high-flying observation planes."

The decision to drop leaflets was done for humanitarian reasons, but they never mentioned the atomic bomb or any special weapon. Although we dropped hundreds of thousands of these leaflets and advised the people to flee from these cities, it does not appear that these reached very many people. Lifton says in his book, *Death in Life,* that he only spoke to one person in his interviews who remembered seeing one. As a child, he had picked one up and took it to his parents, but they dismissed it as mere propaganda.

This question of leaflets bothered me. I had heard it said that we dropped leaflets over Hiroshima before the bomb was dropped. From newspaper accounts, I have found this did not happen. We have been criticized because we did not employ the same humanitarian concern for Hiroshima as we did for other cities we bombed.

During the last week before the nuclear bombing, squadrons of b-29s were making daily attacks on the Japanese mainland, dropping thousands of bombs and reducing cities to rubble. I seriously believe that, had the b-29s continued their daily raids on the cities, the war would have been over very quickly. How long could any country hold out under such pressure? The naval blockage had cut off supply routes and we know from our story that food was already scarce. The Japanese cabinet knew that the armed forces had been desperately short of fuel for almost a year.

From *No High Ground:*

"As early as the fall of 1944 the (Japanese) Navy was so
pinched that some of the warships lost in the Philippine Sea
battles might not have been able to return to their home ports
even if they had escaped from the American bombs and
torpedoes."

The Japanese army was making shell cases out of dull gray substi-
tute metals; there wasn't any more brass. The country had used all of
its metal resources and was giving the soldiers bullets made from bamboo and equipping them with *bamboo spears* to fight the expected
invasion. When soldiers went on leave to visit their families, they were
told to scrounge around and bring any available metal back with them
to be melted down for bullets. The bamboo spears were also to be the
principal weapons of the "National Volunteer Fighting Corps," a sort
of last-ditch home guard into which every Japanese male would soon
be mobilized. I wonder if this was any more "volunteer" than the
forcible drafting of the men, the women working in the factories, or
the school children helping to destroy houses for firebreaks?

Every foot of the shoreline was being prepared for defense, but in
most cases this meant only barbed wire because there was little cement
for fortification. Fighting would be done from caves in the hills
because they knew they could not defend the beaches. The navy had
finally adopted the *kamikaze* tactics of the air force as a last ditch effort.
In July, 700 small craft, loaded with explosives and intended for one-
way voyages only, were being prepared for use against u.s. invasion
fleets. Even propaganda reflected the hopelessness of the situation,
telling the people to be ready to "die in honor." Hindsight is a won-
derful thing. From this point in history, we have access to both sides
of the story.

My research disclosed another disturbing fact. As early as July,
1945, Japan was trying to find a way to surrender. It was not unani-
mous—there were still some holdouts among the staunch military
leaders—but leading Japanese were attempting to end the war before
their country suffered total devastation. Allen W. Dulles, supervisor
of oss operations in conquered Germany, was approached through an

intermediary with a Japanese surrender proposal. At the same time, Japan was also trying to get Russian officials to act as intermediaries for them. The Russians were not anxious to cooperate and did not pass the messages along. It is now known that Russia was sitting on the fence, unwilling to commit themselves either way. One author said they were delaying entry into the Pacific war until we had done all the "dirty work." They were waiting to see where they could get the best spoils of war. Russia officially declared war on Japan the day *after* the A-bomb was dropped, so these accusations were probably true.

The Emperor himself was the one who was pushing for the Russians to act as surrender intermediaries. He wished to relieve his people of the suffering, and wanted the war to be ended as swiftly as possible. He had never been in favor of war. It had been ordered by the military elements of his government. During July, 1945, he sent a special envoy to Moscow to ask their help, even offering them property concessions if they would intercede. The Russians refused to see the envoy and left for the Potsdam Conference. The Japanese didn't know that Russia wasn't interested in helping a loser.

From *The Atomic Bomb and the End of World War II* by Herbert Feis:

> "Their reliance on the good-will of the Soviets up to the end was one of the main causes of the ultimate Japanese tragedy."

The main condition of the Japanese surrender terms was that they be allowed to keep the Emperor as head of their government. This was very important to them. They considered him a deity as well as leader. Japan insisted they could not agree to an unconditional surrender unless this one important concession were included. Without this, they had no alternative but to fight to the last man in an all-out effort.

People might way that we were probably ignorant of these surrender feelers being sent out and therefore we were not at fault. But the truth is that we *did* know. We had broken the Japanese codes long before and were intercepting and monitoring these messages. Our government was fully aware that the Japanese were trying to surrender and we knew the question of the Emperor was the most important item. These facts were even mentioned in the New York *Times* during July, 1945. Many American leaders were in favor of letting the Emperor remain as leader of the country. They thought in this way the scattered armies would surrender if told to and the transition of the country to a peaceful status would be easier.

One authority thought the Japanese government might be searching for some excuse to surrender. He suggested having representatives meet somewhere on the China coast and discuss these things.

On July 16, the first plutonium bomb was tested near Alamogordo, New Mexico. It was extremely successful, even vaporizing the hundred-foot tower on which the bomb rested. But it was insisted that the final test would have to be a "battle test." The effects of exploding a bomb over a populated city and the radiation it would release were still unknown, the subject of theory and speculation. There had been a time during experimentation when scientists feared that an exploding atomic bomb might ignite the nitrogen in the air and the hydrogen in the oceans and consume the earth. Their fears were partly laid to rest by more calculations, but this shows the uncertainty of what the bomb was capable of doing. No one on the face of this earth really knew. No man had any way of knowing that a new disease—radiation sickness—would also be spawned, whose total effects would not be known for generations.

When General Dwight D. Eisenhower was finally told about the bomb, he said he hoped it would not have to be used because he hated to see the U.S. be the first to employ a weapon with such incredible potential for death and destruction. By this time, six U.S. war leaders had expressed reservations about the use of the bomb. They were overridden by a score of influential White House advisers, plus Truman's committee and many top scientists.

Nagasaki was added to the list, even though it was thought not to be an ideal target. It lay in hilly terrain unsuited for a full demonstration of the bomb's power and had already been attacked by conventional bombs. Photos showed that an Allied prisoner of war camp was located one mile north of the center of Nagasaki. The War Department said it would make no difference since there were prison camps in practically every major Japanese city. Visual bombing would be very important in order to select specific targets within the cities on the list.

On July 26, another ultimatum was sent to Japan telling her to surrender unconditionally or face "prompt and utter destruction." No mention was made of the atomic bomb. Secretary of War Stimson urged that a statement be included in the ultimatum to the Japanese that where was no danger to their Emperor and they could continue this form of government if the people so wished. He was over-ridden and this part was left out of the message. Why? This requirement was eventually allowed at the end of the war. The reaction in Japan was instant, they could not accept the ultimatum because it made no mention of the future status of the Emperor. It is odd how small details often write the outcome of history. This was Japan's last chance. Truman would say no more until the bomb fell.

During the Potsdam Conference, Stalin told Truman about the Japanese proposals for mediation, but that he considered their terms of surrender "too vague." Because of what Stalin said, and because he thought the Japanese had rejected the ultimatum outright, Truman decided to go ahead with the plans for using the A-bomb. Simple misunderstandings on all sides had combined together to strike the death blow to Japan.

The "Enola Gay," the B-29 that had been chosen to drop the world's first atomic bomb, was on Tinian Island and plans were proceeding for the attack. There would be seven planes involved. Three would leave first and fly over the three cities on the list and report the weather conditions. Because the bomb had to be dropped visually, it was essential that there be clear weather. Two more B-29s would escort Commander Tibbets' "Enola Gay" to the target. One of these would carry scientists with instruments to measure the blast and the other plane would carry cameras. A seventh plane would fly to Iwo Jima, less than halfway, and stand by for a transfer of the bomb in case Tibbets' plane developed engine trouble.

The aiming point in Hiroshima was near the Japanese Second Army Corps headquarters, but the radius of damage was expected to include almost the entire city, save the dock area. This would eliminate many of the city's factories that were located in that area. The explosion would occur in the air, 1,850 feet above ground. The scientists believed this would reduce radioactivity to a minimum, but they weren't sure, so they ordered that no friendly aircraft be within a 50-mile radius.

President Truman's military advisors told him the bomb might kill only 20,000 people, assuming that air-raid shelters were being used. They had no way of knowing that the people were not using the shelters because we had cried "wolf" too often. They also had no way of foreseeing that there would be no alarm sounded that morning and the vast majority of the people would be on the streets.

At 7:09 A.M., the weather plane, "Straight Flush," flew over the outskirts of Hiroshima at the same time the other weather planes were flying over the other target cities. The plane made a full turn and came back across the city from the opposite direction and headed out to sea at 7:25 A.M. The only air-raid alert sounded was when this plane flew over the city. Quote from *No High Ground:*

> "Not a single Japanese fighter had risen to challenge it and the few bursts of flak had puffed harmlessly two miles below the plane."

This is what Nogorigatu said about the defenses of the city.

All of the cities on the list were having good weather conditions, but Tibbets decided to go for Hiroshima. It had been the first choice anyway because it was the most untouched of the three targets. At the time the decision was made, the "Enola Gay" was over the Japanese mainland. No one knew until that moment which city was to be chosen for this dubious honor. There was no time for warning of any kind. The "Enola Gay" also met no opposition or flak as it flew over the city. At 8:15 A.M., the bomb was released and the planes had to make tight turns and get out fast. The other planes dropped bundles containing instruments and cameras that descended by parachutes.

The visual effects of the bomb's damage were later reported to be greater than any test could have predicted. Several factors combined by chance to produce even more devastation than had been expected. First was the time of the explosion. All over Hiroshima, thousands of charcoal braziers that were the stoves in most households were still full of hot coals after breakfast cooking. The massive blast wave that followed the explosion knocked over these stoves and added to the huge fire that spread out far beyond the original blast area, destroying the wood-and-paper houses. Second, the all-clear had sounded after the "Straight Flush" turned out to sea, and people were on their way to work. No new alert was sounded when the "Enola Gay" flew over with her deadly cargo. It was a fact that small formations of planes had flown over many times before without dropping bombs, so the people were not worried. These were some of the factors that the scientists believed added to the amount of casualties. Also the radiation, which scientists had thought would not reach the ground in such deadly doses, made the bomb unexpectedly lethal.

When the leaders of Japan found out what had happened, they were convinced that possession of the atomic bomb by the u.s. meant the war was over. This would give them a good excuse to end the war without "losing face." They would not have to blame the military, the manufacturing or anyone else ... just the atomic bomb. It was an excellent way out of the mess they had created. The army was not so easily convinced; they played it down in the news releases. They wanted to be sure it was an atomic bomb and not just a huge conventional one. They flatly refused to consider surrender until they had conducted an investigation in Hiroshima. They demanded that the truth be kept from the people as long as possible. The Japanese were told they must fight on for their Emperor. But the people of Hiroshima, if they could overcome their pain on that second day of the atomic age, were more concerned with finding their loved ones than with battling for their Emperor. When the first observers arrived on the scene they were horrified and said this was destruction like none other ever seen in war. Finally convinced, they became desperate for surrender, and the plans were rapidly made ready. But it was too late, for the death knell had already sounded for Nagasaki.

Truman promised to destroy much of Japan if her leaders did not surrender. He said they could "expect a rain of ruin from the air, the like of which has never been seen on this earth." Only three days after the bombing of Hiroshima, the bomb was dropped on Nagasaki, killing 40,000 and injuring 60,000. It also destroyed a p.o.w. camp, killing at least 16 prisoners. But strangely, if the bombardier had erred about three miles south, he would have destroyed a larger p.o.w. camp containing more than 1400 allied prisoners that military intelligence did not even know existed. Another bomb was planned for Tokyo.

Quote from *Hiroshima and Nagasaki Reconsidered* by Barton J. Bernstein:

> "Truman wrote shortly after Nagasaki: Nobody is more disturbed over the use of atomic bombs than I am, but I was greatly disturbed over the unwarranted attack by the Japanese on Pearl Harbor and the murder of our prisoners of war. The only language they seem to understand is the one we have been using to bombard them. When you have to deal with a beast you have to treat him as a beast. It is most regrettable but nevertheless true."

One question that later disturbed Americans concerned not Hiroshima but Nagasaki. Some, who acknowledged the military justification for the first atomic attack, wondered what excuse there was for a repetition of the slaughter three days later, when the Japanese leaders were already moving to surrender and were frantically trying to arrange the means to do so. The answer is no clearer now than it was then. There were only two atomic bombs ready at that time and the original orders to the men on Tinian Island was to keep using the bombs until Japan surrendered. No one changed these orders. The superiors in Washington said they had no knowledge of what was really going on in Japan. Even after Japan offered to surrender on August 10, the Air Force continued conventional bombing. Truman reinstated the attacks after a brief pause to intimidate the Japanese and to demonstrate to other countries (especially Russia) and to the American public the power of the u.s. Air Force. On August 14, in an effort to dramatize our strength, we launched more than 1000 bombers. Today we know the war was really over and Japan was defeated and trying to surrender.

In *No High Ground*, many people involved in the bombing of Hiroshima were later asked how they felt about it. One man said, "What's the difference, one bomb or thousands?" Another said, "It made me angry when it came out that the Japs had been trying to

surrender, but we were afraid of nonsense about unconditional surrender. Since Japan was already beaten, it was a tragic u.s. flub to
needlessly vaporize 140,000 people." One man involved thought it
would have been better to drop one bomb on top of Mount Fujiyama
and blow the top off it. This would have been a powerful show of
strength. Still another said that if the Japs had had an A-bomb they
would have done the same thing to us.

It is a controversy that continues today with no one in a position
to render absolute judgment. Many people saw the killing of 115,000
(*our* figures for both bombings) civilians as justified because it saved
more lives that would have been lost if we had invaded Japan. These
people find it hard to differentiate between the napalm that killed over
78,000 in Tokyo and the A-bomb that killed about the same in Hiroshima. Only the methods were different. The results were the same:
death to many innocent civilians. Some have said that the sacrifice of
Hiroshima would not be in vain because it showed that the new
weapons' threat was so great that the world could not possibly afford
another war. This has been true to a certain extent, we have never had
another world-wide war and the bomb has been a constant threat that
hangs by a thread over the heads of the human race. But for how long?
These memories are fading into the past and there are those today who
speak of the possibly of surviving limited nuclear war. It has been said
that there is not a single world leader today who has even seen an
atomic explosion. If they could only once witness the awesome power
that would be unleashed, would they talk so confidently?

Of course these are only my opinions and I may be grossly mis-
judging those involved. But it does make one wonder. It would be a
terrible pity if all those people died not because of the authorities
wanting to end the war quickly, but because they were guinea pigs in
a massive, expensive scientific experiment. I have no answers, no
solutions, only questions.

At the time in America, protests against the atomic attacks were
few and came mostly from pacifists, opponents of the war, clergymen
and scientists. Albert Einstein, among others, argued that the bomb
was an inhumane weapon, its use was not necessary to end the war
and it might launch an arms race with the Soviet Union. (He
co-authored a book with Sigmund Freud in 1933 entitled *Why War?*)

Ex-president Herbert Hoover agreed privately that the war could have been ended without the bomb and wrote that its use "with its indiscriminate killing of women and children, revolts me."

Most Americans rejoiced that the costly war had finally ended. Few had serious moral or political doubts about the decision to use the bomb as a combat weapon. But how many then or even today fully understand what had happened? All they cared about was that the long war was finally over and that their lives could return to normal. They were not looking backward but forward. It was only in recent times that people had time to reflect upon what had happened.

I know we needed to end the war before any more of our men were killed. It was true, there were many war atrocities. It was a horrible and ruthless war and needed to be brought to a close so we could get on with the business of living. But did we need to do it that way? Was revenge made the sweeter by taking so many innocent lives? It has been said that war is hell, and I believe war does make monsters of us all. I think it boils down to what Nogorigatu said, "The governments make the wars, not the people." True, if it were up to the people of a country, no war would ever be necessary. They are merely swept up and carried along. Our Japanese friend also said, "No one wins! No one *ever* wins!"

On February 2, 1958, Ex-president Truman was being interviewed by Edward R. Murrow on television. The following is a segment from that broadcast that was reproduced in the New York *Times* and quoted in Robert J. Lifton's *Death in Life:*

> " 'Any regrets?' Mr. Murrow asked.
> " 'Not the slightest—not the slightest in the world,' Mr. Truman responded. He stated that the alternative would have been an invasion in which casualties probably would have run to a half million. 'And when we had this powerful new weapon, I had no qualms about using it because a weapon of war is a destructive weapon. That's the reason none of us want war and all of us are against war. But when you have the weapon that will win the war, you'd be foolish if you didn't use it.' He expressed the hope that the 'new and terrible hydrogen weapon' would never be used. 'If the world gets

into turmoil, however,' he continued, 'it will be used. You can be sure of that.' "

Quote from *The Atomic Bomb and the End of World War II:*

"Fifteen years afterwards, General Hap Arnold included this statement in his report to the Secretary of War: 'Even before the atomic bomb mass air raids were obliterating the great centers of mankind, the Twentieth Air Force was destroying Japanese cities at a cost to Japan 50 times the cost to us. Atomic bombing is even more economical. Destruction is too cheap, too easy. No effort spent on international cooperation will be too great if it assures the prevention of this destruction.' "

I think this quote from *No High Ground* sums up my feelings perfectly. Chaplain William B. Downey was stationed on Tinian Island when the "Enola Gay" took off and he later said:

"The quantity of killing is not the issue. The wrong is the killing, whether by fire bombs from hundreds of planes, by one atomic bomb or by a single rifle bullet. War itself is the evil that man must conquer."

I started out with an interesting experiment in reincarnation regressive hypnosis and found instead a powerful anti-war statement delivered from beyond the grave. Was this the purpose of the memory being awakened in Katie, so that this statement could be brought to the world? I learned much from the reliving of Nogorigatu's suffering. Will our world learn anything from it? What do we say to the dead? What do we say to those who died then and those who may die in the future, if the world continues on this path?

No matter what side of the nuclear fence someone is sitting on, I hope my story has at least opened some eyes to the horrible possibilities of a nuclear war—a war that only hurts the innocent. Maybe within this regression account there is a lesson for humanity. If so, then all these people would not have died in vain. I am glad that one of them chose to reincarnate in a body that I would have contact with and that he chose to haunt us until the story was finally put on paper. I came to know him and to love him. May he now rest in peace and may Katie continue with her life at last free of this terrible burden. It will never bother her again, she has passed it on to *us!*

What will *we* do with it?

Bibliography

BERNSTEIN, BARTON, J., *Hiroshima and Nagasaki Reconsidered,* New Jersey, General Learning Press, 1975.

FEIS, HERBERT, *The Atomic Bomb and the End of World War II,* New Jersey, Princeton University Press, 1961, 1966.

HACHIYA, M.D., MICHIHIKO, *Hiroshima Diary,* North Carolina, University of North Carolina Press, 1955.

HERSEY, JOHN, *Hiroshima,* New York, Knopf Publishers, 1946.

"Japan," *Collier's Encyclopedia.*

KNEBEL, FLETCHER, and BAILEY II, CHARLES W., *No High Ground,* New York, Harper and Brothers, 1960.

LIFTON, ROBERT J., *Death in Life,* New York, Random House, 1967.

MOORE, W. ROBERT, "Face of Japan," *National Geographic,* December 1945.

New York *Times,* August 1945.

United States Government Printing Office, *Mission Accomplished,* Washington, D.C., 1946.

About the Author

Photo by Richard Quick.

DOLORES CANNON was born in 1931 in St. Louis, Missouri. She was educated and lived in Missouri until her marriage in 1951 to a career Navy man. She spent the next 20 years traveling all over the world as a typical Navy wife and raised her family.

In 1968 she had her first exposure to reincarnation via regressive hypnosis when her husband, an amateur hypnotist, stumbled across the past life of a woman he was working with (outlined in her book *Five Lives Remembered*). At that time the "past life" subject was unorthodox and very few people were experimenting in the field. It sparked her interest, but had to be put aside as the demands of family life took precedence.

In 1970 her husband was discharged as a disabled veteran, and they retired to the hills of Arkansas. She then started her writing career and began selling her articles to various magazines and newspapers. When her children began lives of their own, her interest in regressive hypnosis and reincarnation was reawakened. She studied the various hypnosis methods and thus developed her own unique technique which enabled her to gain the most efficient release of information from her subjects. Since 1979 she has regressed and cataloged information gained from hundreds of volunteers. She calls herself a regressionist and a psychic researcher who records "lost" knowledge. She has also worked with the Mutual UFO Network (MUFON) for a number of years.

Her published books include *Conversations with Nostradamus* (3 volumes), *Keepers of the Garden, Conversations with a Spirit,* and *Jesus and the Essenes* (published by Gateway Books in England). She has written several other books (to be published) about her most interesting cases including another title from Gateway entitled *They Walked with Jesus.*

Dolores has four children and thirteen grandchildren who demand that she be solidly balanced between the "real" world of her family and the "unseen" world of her work. If you wish to correspond with Dolores about her work, you may write to her at the following address: (Please enclose a self-addressed, stamped envelope for her reply.)

Dolores Cannon, P.O. Box 754
Huntsville, AR 72740-0754